Death and the Labyrinth:

THE WORLD OF
RAYMOND ROUSSEL

Death and the Labyrinth:

THE WORLD OF RAYMOND ROUSSEL

MICHEL FOUCAULT

Translated from the French by Charles Ruas

WITH AN INTRODUCTION BY JOHN ASHBERY

Doubleday & Company, Inc., Garden City, New York
1986

Library of Congress Cataloging-in-Publication Data
Foucault, Michel.
Death and the labyrinth.
Translation of: Raymond Roussel.
1. Roussel, Raymond, 1877–1933—Criticism and
interpretation. I. Title.
PQ2635.O96168Z6313 1986   848'.91209   85-16265
ISBN 0-385-27854-3

*This translation
is for Christophe de Menil*

ACKNOWLEDGMENTS

Michel Foucault gave his generous assistance to this project. His untimely death makes us realize all that we have lost.

I want to thank John Ashbery for contributing his pioneering essay on Raymond Roussel as the introduction to this volume, as well as for giving us access to his Roussel archives.

In my work I have followed Trevor Winkfield's brilliant translation of *How I Wrote Certain of My Books* by Raymond Roussel. I have also quoted from Kenneth Koch's translation of Canto III of *Nouvelles Impressions d'Afrique*, which is reprinted in the appendix to Trevor Winkfield's translation.

For the novels by Raymond Roussel I relied upon Lindy Foord and Rayner Heppenstall's translation of *Impressions of Africa* (Berkeley and Los Angeles: University of California Press, 1967) and Rupert Copeland Cuningham's translation of *Locus Solus* (New York: Riverrun Press, 1983).

I want to express my gratitude to the following people for their contribution to this project: Juris Jurjevics, Douglas Stumpf, Fran McCullough, Shaye Areheart, Joellyn Ausanka, and most of all Rob Wynne for his unfailing encouragement.

Contents

On Raymond Roussel

BY JOHN ASHBERY

RAYMOND ROUSSEL'S NAME does not yet mean very much in America; it means almost as little in France, where he is remembered as an amiable eccentric, the author of naïve plays which intrigued the surrealists. And yet in spite of the fact that the public has always regarded him as a curiosity, some of France's leading modern writers and artists, from Gide and Cocteau to Duchamp and Giacometti, from the surrealists to the school of the *nouveau roman*, have considered him a genius.

Who was the writer capable of arousing such diverse enthusiasms, and why, in spite of it all, does Roussel remain an obscure figure known only to a few initiates? Perhaps there is a kind of answer in Cocteau's remarks about him in *Opium:* "Raymond Roussel, or genius in its pure state. . . . In 1918 I rejected Roussel as likely to place me under a spell from which I could see no escape. Since then I have constructed defenses. I can look at him from the outside." It is true that there is hidden in Roussel something so strong, so ominous, and so pregnant with the darkness of the "infinite spaces" that frightened Pascal, that one feels the need for some sort of protective equipment when one reads him. Perhaps the nature of his work is such that it must be looked at "from the outside" or not at all.

Though Roussel died only in 1933, at the age of fifty-six, there exists little biographical information about him. What little we do know is contained chiefly in his short memoir published posthumously in *Comment J'ai Écrit Certains de Mes Livres,* and in the articles of Michel Leiris, the leading authority on Roussel. Luckily for us, Leiris, a former surrealist who is one of France's most brilliant and original writers, knew Roussel from childhood, since his father was Roussel's business manager. If it had not been for this fortunate coincidence, our knowledge of Roussel's life would be slight indeed.

Roussel was born on January 20, 1877, in Paris in his parents' apartment at 25 Boulevard Malesherbes. His father, Eugène Roussel, was a wealthy stockbroker; his mother, née Marguerite Moreau-Chaslon, came from a bourgeois family of some prominence. There were two elder children—Georges, who died of tuberculosis in 1901 at the age of thirty, and Germaine, who later married into the nobility, becoming Comtesse de Breteuil, later Duchesse d'Elchingen.

We may suppose for Roussel a Proustian childhood dominated by his possessive and eccentric mother; the Roussels were, in fact, near neighbors of the Prousts, who lived at 9 Boulevard Malesherbes; they had common friends, including the painter Madeleine Lemaire, in whose salon Proust made his debut in society and who painted a portrait of Roussel as a child, and later illustrated his poem *Le Concert* in *Le Gaulois du Dimanche,* as she had illustrated Proust's *Les Plaisirs et les Jours.* Proust and Roussel knew each other— how well, we do not know. There is a reference to a Madame Roussel in Proust's correspondence with his mother, and a passage in a letter from Proust to Roussel, containing polite praise of Roussel's *La Doublure*, included in the publicity brochure which accompanied Roussel's books. The curious similarity between the temperament and work of the two men (Roussel seeming a kind of dark and distorted reflection of Proust) has been noted: Cocteau, for instance, called Roussel "the Proust of dreams."

The Roussels' wealth increased and during the late eighties they moved from the Boulevard Malesherbes to a large *hôtel particulier* off the Champs-Élysées at 50 Rue de Chaillot (now 20 Rue Quentin-Bauchart). When Roussel was thirteen, his mother persuaded his father to let him leave the *lycée* and continue his studies at the Paris Conservatory, where he studied piano with Louis Diémer and won a second and then a first honorable mention. He began to compose songs at the age of sixteen, but gave these up for poetry a year later because he found that "the words came easier than the music."

In 1897, when he was twenty, his first book, a "novel" in verse entitled *La Doublure* (which can mean either "The Understudy" or "The Lining"), was published at his own expense by the firm of Lemerre, known especially for its editions of the Parnassian poets. While he was writing *La Doublure*, Roussel had experienced for several months "a sensation of universal glory of an extraordinary intensity." The complete failure of the book plunged him into a state of violent despair from which he never fully recovered. Later he was treated by the famous psychologist Pierre Janet, who describes him under the name of Martial in his book *De l'Angoisse à l'Extase*. Here is Janet on Roussel: "He lives alone, cut off from the world, in a way which seems sad but which suffices to fill him with joy, for he works almost constantly. . . . He will not accept the least bit of advice; he has an absolute faith in the destiny reserved for him. 'I shall reach the heights; I was born for dazzling glory. It may be long in coming, but I shall have a glory greater than that of Victor Hugo or Napoleon. . . . This glory will reflect on all my works without exception; it will cast itself on all the events of my life: people will look up the facts of my childhood and will admire the way I played prisoner's base. . . . No author has been or can be superior to me. . . . As the poet said, you feel a burning sensation at your brow. I felt once that there was a star at my brow and I shall never forget it.' These affirmations concerning works which do not seem destined to conquer a large public and which have attracted so little attention seem to indicate weakness of judgment or exalted pride—yet Martial merits neither criticism. His judgment on other subjects is quite sound, and he is very modest and even timid in his other conduct."

Embittered by the failure of *La Doublure* and the works which followed it, and no doubt also by the derision that now greeted his rare appearances in Paris society, Roussel began to lead the retired, hermetic existence which Janet mentions. He installed himself in a Second Empire mansion that the family owned in Neuilly at 25 Boulevard Richard Wallace—an elegant, secluded avenue bordering the Bois de Boulogne. Here he worked constantly behind the closed shutters of his villa, which was set among several acres of beautifully kept lawns and flower beds, like the villa Locus Solus in his novel of that same name, the property of a Jules Verne inventor-hero named Martial Canterel, who is of course Roussel himself.

After the First World War, during which he held a relatively safe and simple post, Roussel began to travel widely, sometimes using the luxurious *roulotte* (a kind of prototype of today's "camper") which he had ordered specially constructed. But he did little sightseeing as a rule, preferring to remain in his stateroom or hotel room working. He visited Tahiti because he admired Pierre Loti; from Persia he

wrote to his friend Madame Dufrène that Baghdad re-
minded him of Lecocq's operetta *Ali-Baba:* "The people
wear costumes more extraordinary than those of the chorus
at the Gaîté." As Michel Leiris points out, "Roussel never
really traveled. It seems likely that the outside world never
broke through into the universe he carried within him, and
that, in all the countries he visited, he saw only what he had
put there in advance, elements which corresponded absolutely with that universe that was peculiar to him. . . .
Placing the imaginary above all else, he seems to have experienced a much stronger attraction for everything that was
theatrical, trompe-l'oeil, illusion, than for reality."

In the 1920s Roussel began to write for the theater. He
had already devised a theatrical version of his 1910 novel
Impressions d'Afrique, which had run for a month in 1912. It
seems that he approached the theater because the public
had failed to "understand" the work in its form as a novel.
Roussel apparently believed that there was a concrete, hidden meaning to the work which the spectators might grasp
if they could see it acted out before them. Produced in May
1912, at the Théâtre Antoine, with some of the leading
actors of the day, including Dorival and Duard, *Impressions
d'Afrique* struck the Parisian public as an enormous joke,
though it did attract spectators like Apollinaire, Duchamp,
and Picabia. But Roussel's later plays were fated to receive
much harsher treatment.

Imagining that the failure of *Impressions* was due to his
lack of experience in writing for the stage, Roussel commissioned Pierre Frondaie, a popular pulp-fiction writer of the
Maurice Dekobra variety, to turn his novel *Locus Solus* into a
play. But neither the adaptation, the fashionable Caligari-
esque sets, the expensive costumes by Paul Poiret nor the
"Ballet de la Gloire" and the "Ballet Sous-Marin" which
filled up most of the second act could save the play from the
guffaws of the public and the spleen of the critics. Roussel

and his strangely titled work became the butt of jokes over-
night, and everyone waited with impatient malice for his
next play.

This was *L'Étoile au Front*, which opened on May 5, 1924,
at the Théâtre du Vaudeville. Still undaunted, Roussel had
hoped to attain success at last by writing an original play,
rather than by adapting his novels. But the uproar at the
opening went beyond anything seen previously. The text
was drowned out by the jeers of the public, who threw coins
at the actors; the latter (who included Jean Yonnel, later
doyen of the Comédie Française) moved up to the footlights
and began to argue strenuously with the spectators. But
this time Roussel had his partisans: the surrealists, including Breton, Aragon, Leiris, Éluard, Desnos, and Masson,
who applauded wildly and battled those who had come to
attack the play.

Paul Éluard, reviewing the play in *La Revolution Surréaliste*,
wrote: "The characters are all marked with the same sign;
each is prey of the same imagination, which carries earth
and heaven on its head. All the stories in the world are
woven out of their words; all the stars in the world are at
their foreheads, mysterious mirrors of the magic of dreams
and of the strangest and most miraculous events. Will they
succeed in distracting these insects, who make a monotonous music with their thinking and eating, who hardly listen
to them and cannot fathom the grandeur of their delirium?
Conjurers, they transform pure and simple words into a
crowd of characters overwhelmed by the objects of their
passion. What they hold in their hands is a golden ray, the
blossoming of truth and dignity, of felicity and love. May
Raymond Roussel continue to show us everything which
has not been. We are a small group for whom this reality
alone matters." And Aragon called Roussel a "president of
the republic of dreams."

Such tributes, while gratifying, were far from the universal public adoration for which Roussel believed himself destined. He never mingled much with the surrealists, though they tried in vain to establish friendly relations with him. Sometimes he would receive them politely, but he seems not to have appreciated their work: once when asked his opinion of it, he replied that he found it *"un peu obscur."* His last play, *La Poussière de Soleils,* was produced in 1926. This time the reviews were as hostile as ever, but a note of fatigue had crept into them: the joke was beginning to wear thin. Discouraged, Roussel decided to abandon the theater. He completed and published a long poem, *Nouvelles Impressions d'Afrique,* on which he had been working since 1915, and began a final novel which was published in its unfinished state in the posthumous collection, *Comment J'ai Écrit Certains de Mes Livres* (1935). In the spring of 1933, determined to leave Paris for good, he traveled to Sicily with his companion Madame Dufrène, the only person with whom he ever was at all intimate (though their relationship appears to have been entirely platonic). For several years he had been drugging himself in a vain attempt to recapture *la gloire,* and he had spent some time at the clinic in St.-Cloud where Cocteau was undergoing the treatment he describes in *Opium.* At the Grande Albergo e delle Palme in Palermo Roussel grew increasingly weaker; on one occasion he cut his wrists in the bathtub, and expressed pleasant surprise afterward at "how easy it was to die." On the morning of July 14, 1933, his body was found on a mattress on the floor, close to the door that connected his room with Madame Dufrène's; the causes and circumstances of his death have never been satisfactorily explained.

Roussel's career can be divided with almost ludicrous facility into four periods, each quite different from the others. The first two books consist entirely of rhymed, photographic descriptions of people and objects; the next two are novels in which description again dominates, but here the things described are fantastic scenes or inventions; the two plays which follow are merely collections of anecdotes which the characters recount to each other. The last work published in his lifetime is the intricate poem *Nouvelles Impressions d'Afrique*, whose complex arrangements of parenthetical thoughts prefigure the stories-within-stories of the last, incomplete novel, entitled *Documents pour Servir de Canevas*.

Though the failure of *La Doublure* apparently ruined Roussel's life, we can be thankful that the book did not have the success he had hoped for. Janet says that Roussel considered it his greatest work, and continued writing only to call the attention of the public to this first masterpiece. Actually it is the least interesting of the texts, though it is evident from the first line that we are in the presence of a writer who cannot be judged by ordinary literary standards. In *La Doublure* he starts out to tell a sordid Zolaesque story of a romance between a fifth-rate actor, Gaspard, and a demimondaine, Roberte; their lovemaking is recounted in a way that suggests how François Coppée might have written if he had been influenced by Alain Robbe-Grillet:

> *Sur sa poitrine à la peau blanche des dessins*
> *Compliqués sont formés d'un côté par des veines;*
> *Son corset par devant a ses agrafes pleines*
> *De reflets sur leur cuivre étincelant, plat. . . .*

> On the left side of her bosom, complicated designs
> are formed on the white skin by veins; the flat,
> gleaming copper of the hooks at the front of her
> corset is full of reflections. . . .

Roberte and Gaspard decide to leave Paris for Nice on Roberte's money; at Nice they mingle in the carnival and thereafter the book is given over to a description of the parade: Roussel insists on the trumpery character of the papier-mâché floats, and lavishes his scorn on the sham of the whole spectacle. It is not surprising, of course, that a young, hypersensitive poet would settle on this ready-made symbol of the vanity of appearances. But Roussel's real interest is in the visual aspects of the carnival—its symbolic potential is merely a pretext for mathematically precise description. Just as his exaltation while writing the book and his subsequent despair are the normal reactions of a young poet magnified to an extent where they no longer make sense in terms of ordinary human behavior, so the conventional literary elements in *La Doublure* are distorted past all recognition.

La Vue (1904) is made up of three long poems: *La Vue, Le Concert*, and *La Source*. In the first the narrator describes in incredible detail a tiny picture set in a penholder: the view is that of a beach resembling that of Biarritz, where Roussel spent his summers. The second poem is a description of an engraving of a band concert on the letterhead of a sheet of hotel stationery. In the third the narrator is seated at lunch in a restaurant:

> *Tout est tranquille dans la salle où je déjeune.*
> *Occupant une place en angle, un couple jeune*
> *Chuchote avec finesse et gaieté; l'entretien*
> *Plein de sous-entendus, de rires, marche bien.*

> All is calm in the dining room where I am having lunch.
> A young couple at a corner table are whispering gaily
> and wittily together. Their conversation, full of
> private jokes and laughter, is going well.

The next fifty pages describe a spa pictured on the label of a bottle of mineral water on the narrator's table. Only at the end of the poem do we return to the dining room; the couple *"chuchote toujours des choses qu'on n'entend pas"* (are still whispering things which can't be overheard). Love is even farther out of the picture than it was in *La Doublure;* the poet, like a prisoner fascinated by the appearance of the wall of his cell, remains transfixed by the spectacle before his eyes, which is not even a real scene but a vulgar reproduction. The other poems in the volume end on a similar note of despair for the unattainable world of human relationships; at the end of *La Vue* the objective tone is suddenly dropped as the author evokes *"le souvenir vivace et latent d'un été / Déjà mort, déjà loin de moi, vite emporté"* (the latent, undying memory of a summer / Already dead, already far from me, borne swiftly away). One sees how much the "new novelists," especially Alain Robbe-Grillet, whose title *Le Voyeur* is an intentional allusion to *La Vue*, have learned from Roussel. Their exasperatingly complete descriptions of uninteresting objects originated with Roussel, and so did the idea of a universe in which people are merely objects and objects are endowed with an almost human hostility.

Reality, so very unsatisfactory, has made its last appearance for some time in Roussel's work. In the novel *Impressions d'Afrique* (1910) he turns his attention to "what has not been." Here again the plot of the novel is a pretext for description. A group of Europeans has been shipwrecked off the coast of Africa. Talou, a tribal king, is holding them for ransom. In order to distract themselves until the ransom money arrives, the travelers plan a "gala" for the day of their liberation. Each contributes a number utilizing his or her particular talents, and the first half of the book is an account of the gala, punctuated by a series of executions which Talou has ordained for certain of his subjects who have incurred his wrath. The second half is a logical explanation of the preposterous and fantastic scenes which have gone before.

Locus Solus (1914) recounts a similar chain of events. A prominent scientist and inventor, Martial Canterel, has invited a group of colleagues to visit the park of his country estate, Locus Solus ("Solitary Place"). As the group tours the estate, Canterel shows them inventions of ever-increas-

ing complexity and strangeness. Again, exposition is invariably followed by explanation, the cold hysteria of the former giving way to the innumerable ramifications of the
latter. After an aerial pile driver which is constructing a
mosaic of teeth and a huge glass diamond filled with water
in which float a dancing girl, a hairless cat, and the preserved head of Danton, we come to the central and longest
passage: a description of eight curious *tableaux vivants* taking place inside an enormous glass cage. We learn that the
actors are actually dead people whom Canterel has revived
with "resurrectine," a fluid of his invention which if injected into a fresh corpse causes it continually to act out the
most important incident of its life. This passage, one of the
most unforgettable in Roussel's work and one of many
which are haunted by the idea of death, was written around
the time his mother died, after a long series of family
deaths. (Giacometti, who read *Locus Solus* a number of
times, told me once that Roussel's inventions, and this one
in particular, had directly inspired much of his early work,
including the sculpture *The Palace at 4 A.M.*)

   After completing their tour of Locus Solus, the guests
follow Canterel to the villa for a "joyous dinner," and this
very full day comes to a close.

   In *Locus Solus* and *Impressions d'Afrique*, Roussel used a
method of writing which he describes in *Comment J'ai Écrit
Certains de Mes Livres*. Sometimes he would take a phrase
containing two words, each of which had a double meaning,
and use the least likely meanings as the basis of a story.
Thus the phrase *"maison à espagnolettes"* (house with window
latches) served as the basis for an episode in *Impressions
d'Afrique* about a house (a royal family or house) descended
from a pair of Spanish twin girls. Elsewhere he would transform a common phrase, a book title, or a line of poetry into
a series of words with similar sounds. A line of Victor
Hugo, *"Un vase tout rempli du vin de l'espérance"* was dena-

tured by Roussel into *"sept houx rampe lit Vesper,"* which he developed into a tale of Handel using seven bunches of holly tied with different colored ribbons to compose, on a banister, the principal theme of his oratorio *Vesper.*

Just as the mechanical task of finding a rhyme sometimes inspires a poet to write a great line, Roussel's *"rimes de faits"* (rhymes for events) helped him to utilize his unconscious mind. Michel Leiris says, "Roussel here rediscovered one of the most ancient and widely used patterns of the human mind: the formation of myths starting from words. That is (as though he had decided to illustrate Max Müller's theory that myths were born out of a sort of 'disease of language'), transposition of what was at first a simple fact of language into a dramatic action." Elsewhere he suggests that these childish devices led Roussel back to a common source of mythology or collective unconscious.

Both of the published plays, *L'Étoile au Front* and *La Poussière de Soleils,* are collections of anecdotes. In the former the pretexts are provided by the various curios in a collection; in the latter, by the clues in a treasure hunt which eventually lead to the discovery of a will. The thread of narration is passed from one character to another, resulting in a lilting and oddly dramatic language.

There is, of course, no more attempt at plot or characterization than in the novels. And yet the plays are theatrical in a curious way. The anecdotes cast on the characters who tell them an unearthly glimmer that is like a new kind of characterization. And these stories, cut up and distributed among the speakers, somehow propel us breathlessly forward. The plays are among the strangest and most enchanting in modern literature.

Nouvelles Impressions d'Afrique (1932) is Roussel's masterpiece: a long poem in four cantos which bear the names of African curiosities. Each canto starts off innocently to describe the scene in question, but the narrative is constantly interrupted by a parenthetical thought. New words suggest new parentheses; sometimes as many as five pairs of parentheses $(((((())))))$ isolate one idea buried in the surrounding verbiage like the central sphere in a Chinese puzzle. In order to finish the first sentence, one must turn ahead to the last line of the canto, and by working backward and forward one can at last piece the poem together. The odd appearance which the bristling parentheses give the text is completed by the militant banality of the fifty-nine illustrations which Roussel commissioned of a hack painter through the intermediary of a private detective agency.

The result is a tumultuous impression of reality which keeps swiping at one like the sails of a windmill. The hiccoughing parenthetical passages that accumulate at the beginning and end of each canto tend to subside in the middle, giving way to long catalogues or lists: for example, lists of gratuitous gifts; idle suppositions; objects that have the form of a cross; or others that are similar in appearance but not in size, and which one must be careful not to confuse, such as a pile of red eggs under falling snow on a windless day and a heap of strawberries being sprinkled with sugar. Just as the hazards of language resulted in the strange "rhyming events," here other banal mechanisms create juxtapositions that are equally convincing. The logic of the strange positions of its elements is what makes the poem so beautiful. It has what Marianne Moore calls "mysteries of construction."

Michel Leiris says of the poem, "We find here, transposed onto the level of poetry, the technique of the stories with multiple interlocking episodes *(tiroirs)* so frequent in Roussel's work, but here the episodes appear in the sentences themselves, and not in the story, as though Roussel had decided to use these parentheses to speed the disintegration of language, in a way comparable to that in which Mallarmé used blanks to produce those 'prismatic subdivi-

sions of the idea' which he mentions in the preface to the
Coup de Dés.'' Roussel is the only modern French poet whose
experiments with language can be likened to those of Mallarmé. And there is, in fact, a feeling of disintegration in
Nouvelles Impressions which has been building up ever since
the dangerous accumulations of adjectives in *La Doublure,*
the perilously conserved corpses of *Locus Solus* and the piti-
less chains of anecdotes in the plays (which resulted in a
"theater of cruelty" unlike anything Artaud ever dreamed
of, turning a proper bourgeois audience into a horde of
wild beasts). In *Nouvelles Impressions* the unconscious seems
to have broken through the myths in which Roussel had
carefully encased it: it is no longer the imaginary world but
the real one, and it is exploding around us like a fireworks
factory, in one last dazzling orgy of light and sound.

Many writers, including André Breton and Jean Ferry
(whose *Étude sur Raymond Roussel* is invaluable as a key to
Nouvelles Impressions), have felt that Roussel hid some secret
meaning or message in his work. Breton (in his preface to
Ferry's book) makes a convincing case for Roussel as an
alchemist whose books are coded messages concealing *le
Grand Oeuvre*—the Philosopher's Stone. According to
Breton, the various clues in the treasure hunt in *La Poussière
de Soleils* form a decipherable message, while Michel Leiris
sees an autobiographical "chain" in the illustrations for
Nouvelles Impressions: "Voluntary death: wall of snow and
fire, organ point, ultimate ecstasy, unique way of savoring
—in an instant—*'la gloire.'* " But if it seems possible that
Roussel did bury a secret message in his writings, it seems
equally likely that no one will ever succeed in unearthing it.
What he leaves us with is a body of work that is like the
perfectly preserved temple of a cult which has disappeared
without a trace, or a complicated set of tools whose use
cannot be discovered. But even though we may never be
able to "use" his work in the way he hoped, we can still

admire its inhuman beauty, and be stirred by a language that seems always on the point of revealing its secret, of pointing the way back to the "republic of dreams" whose insignia blazed on his forehead.

POSTSCRIPT

The above essay was written in 1961 and published in *Portfolio and ARTnews Annual* in 1962. Much of the information came from my own research in France at a time when very few people there or elsewhere took Roussel seriously as a writer. (I even gained a brief notoriety in Paris as "that crazy American who's interested in Raymond Roussel.") Since then, Roussel has been rediscovered and is now considered an ancestor of much experimental writing being done today both in Europe and America. Volumes have been devoted to him, notably Michel Foucault's study and a biography by François Caradec, *Vie de Raymond Roussel* (Paris: Pauvert, 1972). The novels *Impressions of Africa* and *Locus Solus* have been published in English translation by the University of California Press; and a collection of posthumous fragments *(Flio)* has appeared in France. In addition to the foregoing essay, I published an article on Roussel's plays in an all-Roussel number of the French review *Bizarre* and a short introduction to an unpublished chapter from his final unfinished novel *Documents pour servir de canevas* in the review *L'Arc* in 1963. At that time the chapter, which I found in Paris, was the first unpublished work of Roussel's to come to light in the thirty years since his death.

In view of the attention Roussel has received in the last decade or so, my introductory essay reprinted here, written before Foucault's book appeared, seems rudimentary. At the time, however, there was nothing on Roussel in English, and therefore I considered my job to be that of identifying and describing him for English-speaking readers. I am happy that others are now examining the texts more closely, encouraged in large part no doubt by Foucault's ground-breaking analysis.

J.A.

Death and
the Labyrinth:

THE WORLD OF
RAYMOND ROUSSEL

1

The Threshold
and the Key

THE WORK IS given to us divided just before the end by
a statement that undertakes to explain how . . . This *How
I Wrote Certain of My Books*, * which came to light after everything else was written, bears a strange relationship to the
work whose mechanism it reveals by covering it in an autobiographical narrative at once hasty, modest, and meticulous.

Roussel seems to respect chronological order; in explaining his work he follows the thread leading directly
from his early stories to the just-published *Nouvelles Impressions d'Afrique* (New Impressions of Africa). Yet the structure
of the discourse seems to be contradicted by its internal
logic. In the foreground, writ large, is the process he used
to compose his early writings; then, in ever-narrowing degrees, come the mechanisms he used to create the novels
Impressions d'Afrique (Impressions of Africa) and *Locus Solus*

* Raymond Roussel, *How I Wrote Certain of My Books*, translated from the French,
with notes, by Trevor Winkfield (New York: SUN, 1975, 1977).

(Solitary Place), which is barely outlined. On the horizon, where language disappears in time, his most recent texts— the plays *La Poussière de Soleils* (Motes in Sunbeams) and *L'Étoile au Front* (Star on the Forehead)—are mere specks. As for the poem *Nouvelles Impressions,* which has retreated to the far side of the horizon, it can be identified only by what it is not. The basic geometry of this "revelation" reverses the triangle of time. By a complete revolution, the near becomes distant, as if only in the outer windings of the labyrinth Roussel can play the guide. He leaves off just as the path approaches the center where he himself stands, holding all the threads at their point of entanglement or— who knows?—their greatest simplicity. At the moment of his death, in a gesture both cautious and illuminating, Roussel holds up to his work a mirror possessed of a bizarre magic: it pushes the central figure into the background where the lines are blurred, placing the point of revelation at the farthest distance, while bringing forward, as if for extreme myopia, whatever is farthest from the moment of its utterance. Yet as the subject approaches, the mirror deepens in secrecy.

The secret is darker still: the solemn finality of its form and the care with which it was withheld throughout the body of his work, only to be given up at the moment of his death, transforms what is revealed into an enigma.

Lyricism is carefully excluded from *How I Wrote Certain of My Books* (the quotations from Dr. Janet that Roussel used to speak about what was undoubtedly the pivotal experience of his life attest to the rigor of this exclusion); there is information in the essay, but no confidences; and yet something definitely is confided through this strange form of the secret that death would preserve and make known. "And I take comfort, for want of anything better, in the hope that perhaps I will have a little posthumous fame with regard to my books." The "how" that Roussel inscribes in the title of his last, revelatory work introduces not only the secret of his language, but also his relationship with such a secret, not to lead us to it, but rather to leave us disarmed and completely confused when it comes to determining the nature of the reticence which held the secret in a reserve suddenly abandoned.

His first sentence, "I have always intended to explain how I wrote certain of my books," clearly shows that his statements were not accidental, nor made at the last minute, but were an essential part of the work and the most constant aspect of his intention. Since his final revelation and original intention now becomes the inevitable and ambiguous threshold through which we are initiated into his work while forming its conclusion, there is no doubt it is deceptive: by giving us a key to explain the work, it poses a second enigma. It dictates an uneasy awareness for the reading of the work: a restless awareness since the secret cannot be found in the riddles and charades that Roussel was so fond of; it is carefully detailed for a reader who willingly lets the cat take his tongue before the end of the game, but it is Roussel who takes the reader's tongue for the cat. He forces the reader to learn a secret that he had not recognized and to feel trapped in an anonymous, amorphous, now-you-see-it-now-you-don't, never really demonstrable type of secret. If Roussel of his own free will said that there *was* a secret, one could suppose that he completely divulged it by admitting it and saying what it was, or else he shifted it, extended and multiplied it, while withholding the principle of the secret and its concealment. Here the impossibility of coming to a decision links all discourse about Roussel with the common risk of being wrong and of being deceived less by a secret than by the awareness that there is secrecy.

In 1932 Roussel sent his printer a portion of the text which would become, after his death, *How I Wrote Certain of*

My Books. It was understood that these pages would not be published during his lifetime. The pages were not awaiting his death; rather, this decision was already within them, no doubt because of the immediacy of the revelation they contained. When, on May 30, 1933, he decided what the structure of the book would be, he had long since made plans never to return to Paris. During the month of June he settled in Palermo, where he spent every day drugged and in an intense state of euphoria. He attempted to kill himself, or to have himself killed, as if now he had acquired "the taste for death which hitherto he feared." On the morning he was due to leave his hotel for a drug cure at Kreuzlingen, he was found dead: in spite of his extreme weakness, he had dragged himself and his mattress against the door communicating with the adjoining room of his companion Charlotte Dufrène. This door, which had been open at all times, was locked from the inside. The death, the lock, and this closed door formed, at that moment and for all time, an enigmatic triangle where Roussel's work is both offered to and withdrawn from us. Whatever is understandable in his language speaks to us from a threshold where access is inseparable from what constitutes its barrier—access and barrier in themselves equivocal since in this indecipherable act the question remains, to what end? To release this death so long dreaded and now so suddenly desired? Or perhaps also to discover anew this life from which he had attempted furiously to free himself, but which he had also long dreamed of prolonging into eternity through his work and through the ceaseless, meticulous, fantastic constructions of the works themselves? Is there any other key, apart from the one in this last text, which is there, standing right up against the door? Is it signaling to open—or motioning to close? Is it holding a simple key which is marvelously ambiguous, ready in one turn either to lock in or to open up? Is it carefully shut on an irrevoca-

ble death, or is it transmitting beyond that death the exalted state of mind whose memory had stayed with Roussel
since he was nineteen and whose illumination he had always sought to recover in vain—except perhaps on this one
night?

It is curious that Roussel, whose language is extremely
precise, said that *How I Wrote Certain of My Books* was a
"secret and posthumous" text. No doubt he meant several
things other than the obvious meaning, which is secret until
death: that death was a ritual part of the secret, its prepared
threshold and its solemn conclusion. Perhaps he meant
that the secret would remain secret even in death, giving it
an added twist, by which the "posthumous" intensified the
"secret" and made it definitive; or even better, death would
reveal that there is a secret without showing what it hides,
only what makes it opaque and impenetrable. He would
keep the secret by revealing that it is secret, only giving us
the epithet but retaining the substance. We are left with
nothing, questioning a perplexing indiscretion, a key which
is itself locked up, a cipher which deciphers and yet is
encoded.

How I Wrote Certain of My Books hides as much, if not more,
than it promises to reveal. It only gives us fragments of a
breakdown of memory, which makes it necessary, as Roussel said, to use "ellipsis." However general his omissions
may be, they are only superficial compared to a more fundamental one, arbitrarily indicated by his simple exclusion,
without comment, of a whole series of works. "It goes without saying that my other books, *La Doublure* [The Lining/
The Rehearsal/The Understudy], *La Vue* [The View/The
Lens/The Vision], and *Nouvelles Impressions d'Afrique*, are
absolutely outside of this process." Also outside of the
secret are three poetical texts, *L'Inconsolable* (The Inconsolable), *Les Têtes de Carton du Carnaval de Nice* (Cardboard
Heads of the Carnival in Nice), and the first poem written

by Roussel, *Mon Âme* (My Soul). What secret underlies his action of setting them aside, satisfied with a simple reference but without a word of explanation? Do these works hide a key of a different nature, or is it the same, but doubly hidden, to the extent of denying its existence? Could there perhaps be a master key which would reveal a silent law to identify the works coded and decoded by Roussel, and those whose code is not to have any evident code? The idea of a key, as soon as it is formulated, eludes its promise, or rather takes it beyond what it can deliver to a point where all of Roussel's language is placed in question.

There is a strange power in this text whose purpose is to "explain." So doubtful is its status, its point of origin, where it makes its disclosures and defines its boundaries, the space that at the same time it upholds and undermines, that after the initial dazzling there is but one effect: to create doubt, to disseminate it by a concerted omission when there was no reason for it, to insinuate it into what ought to be protected from it, and to plant it even in the solid ground of its own foundation. *How I Wrote Certain of My Books* is, after all, one of *his* books. Doesn't this text of the unveiled secret also hold its own secret, exposed and masked at the same time by the light it sheds on the other works?

From this ambiguous situation one could define certain forms for which Roussel's works would provide the models. (Is it not, after all, the secret's secret?) Perhaps beneath the process revealed in this last text, another set of laws governs even more secretly and in a completely unforeseen way. The structure would be exactly that of *Impressions d'Afrique* or of *Locus Solus*. The scenes performed on stage at the Theater of the Incomparables or the machines in the garden of Martial Canterel have an apparent narrative explanation—an event, a legend, a memory, or a book—which justifies the episodes; but the real key—or in any case, another key at a more profound level—opens the text in all its force and reveals, beneath its marvels, the muffled phonetic explosion of arbitrary sentences. Perhaps in the end, his whole body of work is based on this model: *How I Wrote Certain of My Books* has the same function as the second part of *Impressions d'Afrique* and the explanatory narratives of *Locus Solus*, hiding, beneath the pretext of giving an explanation, the underground force from which his language springs.

It could also be that the revelations made in *How I Wrote Certain of My Books* have only a preparatory value, telling a kind of salutary lie—a partial truth, which signifies that one must look further and in greater depth. Then the work would be constructed on multilevels of secrecy, one ordering the other, but without any one of them having a universal value or being absolutely revelatory. By giving us a key at the last moment, this final text would be like a first retrospective of the works with a dual purpose: it opens the structure of certain texts at the level closest to the surface, but indicates for these and the other works the need for a series of keys, each of which would open its own box, but not the smallest, best protected, most precious one contained inside. This image of enclosure is common with Roussel. It is used with great care in *Documents pour Servir de Canevas* (Documents to Serve as Canvas); *La Poussière de Soleils* aptly uses it as a method for discovering a secret. In *Nouvelles Impressions* it takes the strange form of ever-expanding elucidations always interrupted by the parenthesis of a new light shed on the subject. Each light in turn is broken by a parenthesis of another brightness, originating from the preceding one, which is held suspended and fragmented for a long time. This succession of disruptive and explosive lights forms an enigmatic text, both luminous and shadowy, which these ordered openings transform into an impregnable fortress.

This process can serve as the beginning and the ending of the text, which was the function of the identical ambiguous sentences he used in his youth to frame brief narratives. It can form the necessary perimeter while leaving free the core of language, the field of imagination, without needing any key other than its own game. The process would then function to protect and to release. It would delineate a privileged place, beyond reach, whose rigorous outward form would free it from all external constraints. This self-containment would disconnect the language from all contact, induction, surreptitious communication, and influence, giving it an absolutely neutral space in which to fully develop. The process then would not determine the central configuration of the work, but would only be its threshold, to be crossed the moment it is drawn—more a rite of purification than an architectural structure. Then Roussel would have used it to frame the great ritual of his entire work, repeating it solemnly for everyone once he had completed the cycle for himself. The process would encircle the work, only letting the initiated have access into the void and completely enigmatic space of the ritualized work, which is to say, isolated, but not explained. *How I Wrote Certain of My Books* can be likened to the lens of *La Vue:* a minuscule surface that must be penetrated by looking through it in order to make visible a whole dimension disproportionate to it, and yet which can neither be fixed, nor examined, nor preserved without it. Perhaps the process no more resembles the work itself than the small lens does the seascape of *La Vue* which is brought to light, revealed, and held—on condition that its essential threshold is crossed with a glance.

Roussel's "revelatory" text is so reserved in its description of the action of the process in the work, and in turn the text is so verbose in types of deciphering, rites of threshold and lock, that it is difficult to relate *How I Wrote Certain of My*

Books to these particular books and to the others as well. Its positive function of giving an explanation as well as a formula—"It seems to me that it's my duty to reveal it, for I have the impression that writers of the future will perhaps be able to exploit it fruitfully"—quickly becomes a never-ending play of indecision, similar to that uncertain gesture on his last night, when Roussel, at the threshold, wanted perhaps to open the door, perhaps to lock it. In a way, Roussel's attitude is the reverse of Kafka's, but as difficult to interpret. Kafka had entrusted his manuscripts to Max Brod to be destroyed after his death—to Max Brod, who had said he would never destroy them. Around his death Roussel organized a simple explanatory essay which is made suspect by the text, his other books, and even the circumstances of his death.

Only one thing is certain: this "posthumous and secret" book is the final and indispensable element of Roussel's language. By giving a "solution" he turns each word into a possible trap, which is the same as a real trap, since the mere possibility of a false bottom opens, for those who listen, a space of infinite uncertainty. This does not put in question the existence of the key process nor Roussel's meticulous listing of facts, but in retrospect it does give his revelation a disquieting quality.

All these perspectives—it would be comforting to close them off, to suppress all the openings, and to allow Roussel to escape by the one exit that our conscience—seeking respite—will grant him.

André Breton wrote, in *Fronton Virage* (The Wall at the Bend in the Road), "Is it likely that a man outside of all traditions of initiation should consider himself bound to carry to his grave a secret of another order . . . is it not more tempting to assume that Roussel obeyed, in the capacity of an initiate, a word of irrefutable command?" Of course—everything would be strangely simplified then, and the work would close upon a secret whose forbidden nature alone would indicate its existence, essence, content, and necessary ritual. And in relation to this secret all of Roussel's texts would be just so much rhetorical skill, revealing, to whoever knows how to read what they say, the simple, extraordinarily generous fact that they don't say it.

At the absolute limit it could be that the "chain of events" of *La Poussière de Soleils* has something in common— in its form—with the progression in the practice of alchemy, even if there is little chance that the twenty-two changes of scenes dictated by the staging of the play correspond to the twenty-two cards of the Major Arcana in a tarot deck. It is possible that certain outward signs of the esoteric process might have been used as models for the double play on words, coincidence and encounters at the opportune moment, the linking of the twists and turns of the plot, and the didactic voyages through banal objects having marvelous stories which define their true value by describing their origins, revealing in each of them mythical avatars which lead them to the promise of actual freedom.

But if Roussel did use such material, and it is not at all certain that he did, it would have been in the way he used stanzas of *"Au clair de la lune"* and *"J'ai du bon tabac"* in his *Impressions d'Afrique,* not to convey the content through an external and symbolic language in order to disguise it, but to set up an additional barrier within the language, part of a whole system of invisible paths, evasions, and subtle defenses.

Like an arrow, Roussel's language is opposed—by its direction more than by its substance—to an occult language. It is not built on the certainty that there is secrecy, only one secret that is wisely kept silent; on the surface it sparkles with a glaring doubt and hides an internal void: it is impossible to know whether there is a secret or none, or several, and what they are. Any affirmation that a secret

exists, any definition of its nature, dries up Roussel's work
at its source, preventing it from coming to life out of this
void which it animates without ever satisfying our troubled
ignorance. In the reading, his works promise nothing.
There's only an inner awareness that by reading the words,
so smooth and aligned, we are exposed to the unallayed
danger of reading other words which are both different and
the same. His work as a whole, supported by *How I Wrote
Certain of My Books* and all the undermining doubts sown by
that text, systematically imposes a formless anxiety, diverging and yet centrifugal, directed not toward the most withheld secrets but toward the imitation and the transmutation
of the most visible forms: each word at the same time ener-
gized and drained, filled and emptied by the possibility of
there being yet another meaning, this one or that one, or
neither one nor the other, but a third, or none.

2

The Cushions of the Billiard Table

THERE IS a shipwrecked European who is captured by a black chieftain. With a miraculous supply of ink and paper, and using pigeons as messengers, he sends his wife a long series of letters describing savage battles and cannibal feasts, with the chieftain as the loathsome hero. Roussel says it all better and faster: "The white man's letters on the hordes of the old plunderer" (*les lettres du blanc sur les bandes du vieux pillard*).

Now "the white letters on the cushions of the old billiard table" (*les lettres du blanc sur les bandes du vieux billard*) are the printed letters drawn in chalk on the sides of the slightly moth-eaten green felt covering of a large billiard table when, to entertain a group of friends confined in a country house on a rainy afternoon, you have them solve a rebus; but, too inept to draw realistic figures, they are asked only to form coherent words from the letters scattered along the perimeter of the large rectangle.

The infinitesimal but immense distance between these

two phrases will give rise to some of Roussel's most familiar
themes: imprisonment and liberation, exoticism, cryptograms, torture by language and redemption by that same
language, and the sovereignty of words whose enigma con-
jures up scenes like the one of guests silently circling the
billiard table in a sort of dance, in which the phrase tries to
reconstitute itself. All this forms the natural landscape of
Roussel's four major works, the four great texts which ad-
here to the process: *Impressions d'Afrique, Locus Solus, L'Étoile
au Front,* and *La Poussière de Soleils.*

The prisons, the human machines, the tortuous ciphers,
the whole network of words, secrets, and signs issue marvelously from a single fact of language, a series of identical
words with two different meanings, the tenuousness of our
language which, sent in two different directions, is suddenly brought up short, face-to-face with itself and forced
to meet again. Yet it could as easily be said that it has a
remarkable richness, since as soon as this ordinary group of
words is considered, a whole flurry of semantic differences
is released. There are letters (epistolary) and letters
(graphic). There are the green felt cushions, and the howl-
ing savages of the cannibal king. The identity of words—
the simple, fundamental fact of language, that there are
fewer terms of designation than there are things to designate—is itself a two-sided experience: it reveals words as
the unexpected meeting place of the most distant figures of
reality. (It is distance abolished; at the point of contact,
differences are brought together in a unique form: dual,
ambiguous, Minotaur-like.) It demonstrates the duality of
language which starts from a simple core, divides itself in
two, and produces new figures. (It's a proliferation of distance, a void created in the wake of the double, a labyrin-
thine extension of corridors which seem similar and yet are
different.) In their wealth of poverty words always refer
away from and lead back to themselves; they are lost and

found again; they fix a vanishing point on the horizon by repeated division, and then return to the starting point in a perfect curve. The mystified guests must have realized this while going around the billiard table, when they discovered that the straight line of words was identical to their circular path.

Eighteenth-century grammarians well understood this marvelous property of language to extract wealth from its own poverty. In their purely empirical concept of signs, they admired the way a word was capable of separating itself from the visible form to which it was tied by its "signification" in order to settle on another form, designating it with an ambiguity which is both its resource and limitation. At that point language indicates the source of an internal movement; its ties to its meaning can undergo a metamorphosis without its having to change its form, as if it had turned in on itself, tracing around a fixed point (the "meaning" of the word, as they used to say) a circle of possibilities which allows for chance, coincidence, effects, and all the rules of the game.

Let's consult Dumarsais,* one of the subtlest grammarians of the period: "The same words obviously had to be used in different ways. It's been found that this admirable expedient could make discourse more energetic and pleasing. Nor has it been overlooked that it could be turned into a game and a source of pleasure. Thus by necessity and by choice, words are often turned away from their original meaning to take on a new one which is more or less removed but that still maintains a connection. This new meaning is called 'tropological,' and this conversion, this turning away which produces it, is called a 'trope.' " In the space created by this displacement, all the forms of rhetoric come to life—the twists and turns, as Dumarsais would put

* César Dumarsais, *Les Tropes*, 2 vols. (Paris, 1818). The first edition is dated 175–.

it: catachresis, metonymy, metalepsis, synecdoche, antonomasia, litotes, metaphors, hypallage, and many other hiero-
glyphs drawn by the rotation of words into the voluminous
mass of language.

Roussel's experiment is located in what could be called
the "tropological space" of vocabulary. It's not quite the
grammarian's space, or rather it is this same space, but
treated differently. It is not where the canonical figures of
speech originate, but that neutral space within language
where the hollowness of the word is shown as an insidious
void, arid and a trap. Roussel considers this game, which
rhetoric exploited to extend its meaning, as a gap that is
stretched open as wide as possible and meticulously measured. He felt there is, beyond the quasi-liberties of expression, an absolute emptiness of being that he must sur-
round, dominate, and overwhelm with pure invention: that
is what he calls, in opposition to reality, thought ("With me
imagination is everything"). He doesn't want to duplicate
the reality of another world, but, in the spontaneous duality
of language, he wants to *discover* an unexpected space, and
to *cover* it with things never said before.

The forms he will construct above this void will methodically reverse the "elements of style." Style is—according to
the necessity of the words used—the possibility, masked
and identified at the same time, of saying the same thing
but in other ways. All of Roussel's language, in its reversal
of style, surreptitiously tries to say two things with the same
words. The twisting, slight turn of words which ordinarily
allows them to make a tropological "move" that brings into
play their fundamental freedom is used by Roussel to form
an inexorable circle which returns words to their point of
origin by force of his constraining rules.

But to return to our double-faceted sequence, one aspect
black and cannibal from Africa, the other aspect the green
of the billiard cryptogram, they are set down twice like two

series identical in form but as far apart in meaning as is possible. (The approximation of *billard* = *pillard* [billiard = plunderer] will be discussed later. It is obviously not an easy task to proceed in an orderly fashion without looking forward or backward in a body of work so closely bound, so uniform, so economical in means and always self-referring.) This opens a chasm in the identity of language, a void that has to be revealed and at the same time filled. Thus it could as well be said: "A *blanc* (white) to fill with *lettres* (letters) from one *bande* (cushion) to the other." (I am not bringing a new development into play with a third set of meanings for these words; I simply want to highlight the "self-referential," as logicians used to call it, the unique identity which Roussel's works always manifest with vibrancy.) Thus "the two found phrases: it was a matter of writing a tale that could begin with the first and conclude with the second. It was from the resolution of this problem that I drew all my materials." The narrative begins with the illegible scrawl on the billiard table, and without interruption in meaning will end with the airborne epistles.

Nothing is simpler: this rule is applied in the three narratives published between 1900 and 1907—*Chiquenaude* (Snap of the Fingers), *Nanon*, and *Une Page de Folklore Breton* (A Page of Folklore from Brittany), and in the seventeen texts which Roussel claims are "from his early youth." These were not brought out before the posthumous publication of *How I Wrote Certain of My Books*. The date of their composition has not been established, nor whether indeed they were written when Roussel was still very young. Perhaps they were written well before *La Doublure*, which was composed and published around his twentieth year. Written well before all his major works and repeated again by their publication at the time of his death, they would frame all of Roussel's language, showing at once his point of departure and of arrival, rather like the way his homonym sentences bracket the narratives which they compose. The word play *jeunesse = genèse* (youth = genesis), used by Roussel when he speaks about them in his last work, would seem to indicate that their publication at just that moment also refers to their internal structure.

According to his autobiography Roussel gave up music at seventeen "in order to devote myself to writing poetry." From that moment an "obsession with work" overwhelmed him: "I worked, so to speak, night and day, for months, which culminated in my writing *La Doublure.*" Yet all "the texts from early youth" are written in prose. It doesn't seem likely that they were written in the time between his conversion to poetry and the writing, in alexandrine verse, of *La Doublure.*

It seems rather as if Roussel wrote them after "his frightful nervous disorder," following the failure of his first work, during a period he simply describes as "several years [of] prospecting." This is the period between 1898 and 1900. It's as if this crisis, seen perhaps in *La Doublure*—with its play of actors and understudies and their double roles, its cardboard heads, its masks with peering eyes, its dominoes hiding what they reveal—had already defined this distance between repetition and double meaning which would run through all the texts of his early youth and, afterward, all of Roussel's works. The "tropological" space where his process is situated would then be analogous to the idea of a mask. The hollowness that opens within a word would not simply be a property of verbal signs, but a more basic ambiguity, perhaps even more dangerous: it would show that a word, like a gaudy cardboard face, hides what it duplicates, and is separated from it only by the slightest layer of darkness. The double meaning of words would be like the repetition, by the mask on top, of the face. It reveals the same eclipse of being. The narratives with identical sentences thus renew the experiment of *La Doublure:* they make this work the secret point of departure for all his works. "If I'm publishing these texts from my early youth, it's to highlight the genesis of my works. For example, the narrative entitled *Parmi les Noirs* (Among the Blacks), is the embryonic form of my book *Impressions d'Afrique*. Everything I've accomplished since was born of the same process."

It's curious to see how Michel Leiris, in the admirable *Rules of the Game*, uses the same tropological space for an experiment that's related and also opposite (the same game according to another set of rules): in the shifting of words which contaminate things—superimposing them into marvelous and monstrous figures—he tries to grasp the fleeting but inevitable truth about what has occurred. From so many things without any social standing, from so many fantastic civic records, he slowly accumulates his own identity, as if within the folds of words there slept, with nightmares never completely extinguished, an absolute memory. These same folds Roussel parts with a studied gesture to find the stifling hollowness, the inexorable absence of being, which he disposes of imperiously to create forms without parentage or species. Leiris experiences the fullness of this moment as an inexhaustible truth in which he can immerse himself without respite, the same expanse that Roussel's narratives cross as if on a tightrope above the void.

Apparently his essays pose no other problems than those they undertake to resolve. The care with which Roussel explains the configuration is even surprising: more than two pages at the beginning of *How I Wrote Certain of My Books,* then in the middle of the work a return to it, discussing the principle of how the first sentence comes back at the end of the text but loaded with a different meaning, which is clear enough in each of his narratives so that it's unnecessary to repeat it in a didactic way: the process is evident at the level of words and in the most obvious turn of the anecdotes. No doubt this principle is only the visible summit of a whole pyramidal order where each of his tales finds its basic structure. The key sentence, in opening and closing the narrative, opens many other locks. Let's bring to these simple texts the careful scrutiny that Roussel set as an example.

The ambiguous sentence which prescribes the starting point of the narrative—the eponymous sentence—gives rise to several circles which are not identical but crisscross one another as if to form a strange roseate configuration. We know the circle of language that connects the same word to different meanings. Close to it is the circle of time; that's because the initial sentence appears as an enigma. "The white letters on the cushions of the old billiard table formed an incomprehensible grouping." The instant language starts, time stops. Turned to stone, the spectacle is presented not as an effect, but as a sign, a freeze-frame where one cannot tell what action has been stopped, nor at which scene. During this pause an enigmatic figure rises at the threshold of language: a motionless close-up which withholds its own meaning. At the start of the game language functions as if it were denying all meaning, and the point at which this occurs is initially masked by these unusual devices which are still silent: "The coils of the enormous python tightened convulsively around the victim the moment I looked up"; "The palm strokes on the squirting white teat were skillful and regular"; "The part in the hair of Rayon-Vert sparkled in the full August light." Starting from this enigmatic scene (the rupture of time, the opening of a space, the eruption of things into view without horizon, the disorientation by the absence of all reference or proportion), the language begins to weave its threads with a double motion of return and retreat. It's the rapid sweep toward the past, the arc of memory going as far as necessary to return to a completely clear present. We are taken back to the starting point which is now the goal: the eponymous sentence has only to be repeated.

But the moment that time first reasserts itself at the level of language, language becomes entangled in the differences in meaning: at the beginning there is a game of croquet whose goals, striated with colored bands, are at opposite ends of a garden walk, and at the end there is a performing dog who draws evenly spaced vertical lines with multicolored pencils on the white page of a note pad. It's the "amplitude of the interplay between multicolored strokes." An innocent pleasantry. A parlor game. The punishment meted out to schoolboys. Yet between the first and the last sentence something important has occurred to the status of language which is difficult to define and pinpoint.

Must it be said that when the narrative is about to return to the starting point, the words display an ironic burst of zeal, repeating themselves and signaling with a derogatory tone (derogatory since the same note at the same resonance means something different) that the narration has indeed returned to the beginning, and that it is time to fall silent because the purpose of the language is precisely to repeat the past? Or could it be that beneath the language, at the most natural moment of repetition, a stratagem—not entirely mastered even though caused by its own limitations—is introduced, a slight gap which causes the same words to mean something else; and, in the end, is it better to remain silent since it is impossible for language to repeat itself exactly? These two possibilities reinforce each other as open questions; there's an area of doubt where words and their meanings change in an ambiguous relationship to each other, transformed by a slow rotation which prevents the return of meaning from coinciding with the return of language.

The uneasiness is not dispelled since the indecision is

infinite, but systematically reversed in *Nouvelles Impressions:* the sequence of comparisons, similes, distinctions, metaphors, and analogies filters one, monotonous, persistent meaning through countless words and objects, through endless repetitions which affirm, in 415 verses and over 200 examples, that what is big must not be confused with what is small. Thus the meaning is immobilized beneath the endless waves of language. But in Roussel's early works it's just the opposite. The meaning seems to jump by itself from between the solid columns of words which hold up the arch of the narrative at the beginning and at the end. *Nouvelles Impressions* is like a negative image of his early works.

In relation to the declared eponymous sentence, there is an antitext that is not only antimeaning, it is antiexistence, pure negativity. The first sentence (for example, "The coils of the snake") is always about tangible objects; the words are laid directly onto things, or rather spring from them even before their visualization, which always lags behind, bringing only a persistent silent presence to what is said: "The greenish skin of the ripening plum seemed as appetizing as could be wished"; "The spots on the wool of the big five-legged sheep heightened its supernatural appearance." The antisentence expresses what it has to say only through a precautionary ritual, and each elaboration attenuates its existence. It's no longer a concrete language referring to things; it comes, not without solemnity, from one of the characters in the story, generally the narrator. Perhaps in order to achieve a repetition he needs a protagonist (like Martial Canterel). The transition from the initial sentence to the antisentence is like going from a performance to back stage, from word-object to word-rejoinder. The result is even more effective because the sentence being repeated no longer refers to things themselves but to their reproductions: sketch, cryptogram, enigma, disguise, theatrical performance, a spectacle seen through glasses, symbolic image. The verbal doubling is carried on at the level of repetition. This exact repetition, this faithful double, this repetition of language has the function of pointing out all the flaws, of highlighting all the impediments to its being the exact representation of what it tries to duplicate, or else of filling the void with an enigma that it fails to solve. The antisentence states the ordered and completed text formed by the letters of white chalk drawn helter-skelter on the cushions of the billiard table. It shows what is missing in these letters, what is hidden as well as what can be glimpsed through them, their black negative and also their positive and clear meaning: the white letters. . . . This antisentence also states that the illustrator did not draw in evenly the spotted mesh on the scales of the fish, that the raindrops on the cook's umbrella fell with unbelievable violence, etc. It's as if the function of this doubled language was to insert itself in the minute separations between the imitation and what it imitates, to bring out the flaws and duplicate that imitation to its greatest extent. Language is a thin blade that slits the identity of things, showing them as hopelessly double and self-divided even as they are repeated, up to the moment when words return to their identity with a regal indifference to everything that differs. This fissure through which is inserted the repetition of words is an aspect of language itself, the stigma of the power it exerts on objects, and by which it wounds them. The last sentence, which denounces the flaw in the duplication of things, repeats the first sentence with only one difference, which produces the shift of meaning in the form: the enigma of the chalk signs on the cushions of the *billiard table* is covered over with the letters of the European on the hordes of the *plunderer*. There are approximately sixteen others of a quality no less deplorable: *le pépin du citron* (the lemon seed), *le pépin du mitron* (the baker boy's infatuations);

the hook, the pike, the bell, idle chatter; the position of the red buttons on the masks of the handsome blond favorite; the position of the red buttons on the Basques, etc.

This minute morphological difference—they are always present and there's only one per sentence—is essential for Roussel. It serves as the organizing principle to the whole: "I would choose two nearly identical words (suggesting the metagram). For example, *billard* and *pillard.* Then I would add similar words, selected for two different meanings, and I would obtain two identical sentences."

The repetition is sought and found only in this infinitesimal difference which paradoxically induces the identical; and just as the antisentence is introduced through the opening created by a minute difference, it is only after an almost imperceptible shift has taken place that its identical words can be set. Both the repetition and the difference are so intricately linked, and adjusted with such exactitude, that it's not possible to distinguish which came first, or which is derived. This meticulous connection gives his polished texts a sudden depth wherein the surface flatness seems necessary. It's a purely formal depth beneath the narrative which opens a play of identity and differentiation that is repeated as if in mirrors. It goes continuously from objects to words, losing track of itself, but always returning as itself. There is the slightly different identity of the inductor words, a difference masked by the identical adjacent words, an identity which covers a difference of meaning, a difference that the narrative tries to eliminate in the continuum of its discourse. This continuity leads to these inexact reproductions whose flaws enable the identical sentence to be introduced; an identical sentence but slightly different. And the simplest, most conventional everyday language, a rigorously flat language which has the function of repeating with exactitude objects and the past for everyone, on entering into the play of infinite multiplication of reflections, is captured, without escape, in the depth of a mirror. The way out goes deeper into an empty labyrinthian space, empty because it loses itself there. When the language rejoins itself, it is shown that the same things are not the same, not here, but other and elsewhere. And this game can always begin again.

The metagram, treated like a game, is thus drawn back from and marginal to everything that's commonplace, settled, and peacefully familiar in the language; it brings forth on a mocking surface the game of continually changing repetitions, and of changes that end up as the same thing, a game where language finds the space it needs. The metagram is both the truth and the mask, a duplicate, repeated and placed on the surface. At the same time, it is the opening through which it enters, experiences the doubling, and separates the mask from the face that it is duplicating.

That's no doubt the reason why of all the works from this period, Roussel was satisfied only with *Chiquenaude*. It's necessary to give a summary of this strange narrative without getting too lost in the inextricable play of double images, repetitions, and impediments.

One evening a music-hall comedy is being performed, but it's not opening night (it's the repetition of the reproduction). The spectator who is going to narrate the play has composed a poem which will be recited several times on stage by one of the characters. But the famous actor who has the part has fallen ill: an understudy will replace him. Thus the play begins with *"les vers de la doublure dans la pièce de Forban talon rouge"* (the verses of the understudy in the play of Red Claw the Pirate). This Mephisto twice removed appears on stage and recites the poem referred to above: a vainglorious ballad in which he boasts of being protected from harm by a piece of magical scarlet clothing that no sword can pierce. In love with a beautiful girl, one night he disguises himself—a new imitation—as her lover, a high-wayman and an inveterate duelist. The bandit's protective genie, his clever alter ego, discovers the devil's plan in the reflections of a magic mirror which unmasks the impersonator by repeating his image; he then takes the magical garment and sews inside it a lining made from a piece of moth-eaten material of the same color, a flawed lining. When the bandit returns to challenge the devil to a duel, confronting his double played by an understudy, he has no trouble piercing the formerly invulnerable material with his blade, now separated and severed from its power by an imitation, to be exact, *"les vers de la doublure dans la pièce du fort pantalon rouge"* (the moth holes in the lining of the material of the strong red pants).

In this text are all the elements which will figure in the works of Roussel: narrated theater; lovers taken by surprise; magical substances; people disguised beyond all proportion as minuscule objects (the corps de ballet as spools, needles, and thread); and also in a general way, it articulates the impossible by amassing evidence with the most meticulous attention to detail. But probably the satisfaction Roussel felt about this text came from the marvelous composition of echoes which reverberate from his beginning, two almost identical sentences which must be connected within the text and in all the configurations that are to be found there: repetition, doubles, their reappearance, impediments, imperceptible differences, divisions, and fatal wounds. It's as if the form imposed on the text by the rules of the game took on its own being in the world acted out and imitated on stage; as if the structure imposed by language became the spontaneous life of people and things. The movement of repetitions and transformations, their constant imbalance, and the loss of substance experienced by words along the way are becoming, surreptitiously, marvelous mechanisms for creating beings; the ontological power of this submerged language.

There is one fact: of all the texts from this period *Chiquenaude* is the only one in which the metagram coincides with the dislocation of the eponymous sentence: *Forban talon rouge, fort pantalon rouge.* This is the formula of the general process as it is applied in *Impressions d'Afrique* and *Locus Solus.* I would also be ready to bet that within the text itself there is something like a model of the double meaning of words which would subsequently become the essential element of his technique. Certain unusual junctures, such as *l'étoffe-fée* (fairy-cloth), *la réserve* (the reserve), *l'enfer* (hell), and *complet magique* (magic suit), ring strangely like the repetition of invisible words which, loaded with another meaning, will circulate beneath the text to order its conjunctions and recognitions. *Chiquenaude* is the only text in the works of Roussel where the process is used, in a unique repetition, in both of its forms: the return of the initial sentence and the tenuous coming together of words which have no natural relationship except in another frame of reference or in a slightly modified form.

Roussel, with surprising vehemence (he was replying to a hypothesis by Vitrac), has denied any relationship between *Chiquenaude* and *La Doublure.* He had a specific reason: *Chiquenaude* is a text already invested completely with the process; all of its nervous system has been drawn in by him, well beyond the principle of repeated sentences. In spite of everything there is a relationship between the disappointing experience of the mask as it is found in *La Doublure* and the play of repetition where the tenets of his youth are found, as well as lost. The mask that reproduces the face by an apparent illusion and which, in its oversized cardboard distortion, with its flaws and peeling colors and black eyeholes, shows itself as a true and false double; the language which scans it meticulously spells out its imperfections, and slides into the space that separates it from the person whom it imitates and who, in turn, is its double. Aren't these already like a first formulation of the profound void underlying objects and words, over which moves the language of the process of doubling itself, experiencing in this trajectory its own disappointing reproduction? *Chiquenaude* is a magical gesture which, in one motion, opens the seam and reveals about language an unsuspected dimension into which it will throw itself. As in all of Roussel's work, this chasm holds between its symmetrical parentheses a cycle of words and objects which are self-generated, and completes its movement with self-efficiency. As nothing outside can disturb the purity and glory enclosed, it finds itself in a repetition which—whether by essential fate or by sovereign will—means the elimination of the self.

These genesis-texts, fecund texts, already promise the end when they will be repeated, the end which is a willed death and a return to the first threshold.

3
Rhyme and Reason

I REALIZE THAT my progress is halting: trying to explain these first attempts in terms of what the form would become in the future; by skipping over *La Doublure*, yet still referring to it in spite of Roussel's prohibition (I will keep my analysis of it for the end, when the circle will have to be completed); neglecting *La Vue*, *Le Concert* (The Concert), and *La Source* (The Source), which are contemporary with the period under study (but to deal with them would mean a detour); relying on his posthumous explanation as my bible, but constantly supplying material which seems to be everywhere at hand, until I am caught up in his explanation of the texts. No doubt I'm exhausting everyone's patience by annotating, all told, pages 4 and 5 of *How I Wrote Certain of My Books*.

A strictly accurate linear development becomes necessary now that we are at the threshold whose seriousness Roussel did not attempt to hide: "At last, when I was about thirty, I felt as though I had finally found my way." It's the period (just after the cyclical tales *Nanon* and *Une Page du Folklore Breton*) when he wrote *Impressions d'Afrique* in a style derived from his previous technique. It's the same slightly monotonous voice as in the early narratives, the same exact words, stretched and flat. Yet it seems to me that it's no longer the same language speaking, that the *Impressions d'Afrique* was born on another verbal continent. The fragile and persistent vessels we already know have taken to this second land those words that prowl around the confines of Roussel's work: "The white letters on the cushions of the old billiard table."

Could it be said that these clear signs written on a dark ground along the length of a familiar game table are the visual representation of the experiment with language Roussel conducted throughout the whole of his work? Could it be a sort of negative code at the boundaries of the realm where language exerts its playful and calculable potential? This would give that phrase the privileged role of conveying the treasure of which, by its meaning, it is the rather clearly drawn outline. The negative copy is one of Roussel's familiar themes: it can be found in the white drawings and the black wax of the sculptor Jerjeck; or even in the negative, as in the example of woven material seen right side out by the *"métier à aubes"* (work at dawn/paddle-wheel loom). These white signs say what they have to say, and yet refute it by their very clarity.

"As for the genesis of *Impressions d'Afrique*, it occurs in the association of the word *billard* (billiard table) with the word *pillard* (plunderer). The plunderer is Talou; the *bandes* are his warrior hordes; the white man is Carmichael (the word "letters" was dropped). Then, amplifying the process, I sought new words related to the word *billard*, always with the intention of using them in a sense other than the obvious one, and each time something new was created. Thus *queue* (billiard cue/train) provided Talou's robes with a train." Sometimes a billiard cue has an initial on it, the initial of its owner: whence the initial (number) on the aforementioned train; the same technique for *bandes* (hordes) and *blanc* (white). "Once outside the realm of *billard,* I continued to use the same method. I selected a word and linked it to another with the preposition *à* (to); and these two words, understood in some other way than their original meaning, provided me with a new creation. . . . I must say that at first this was difficult work."

That isn't hard to believe. Nor is it easy—even though strictly speaking there may be no common standard—to provide a detailed analysis of this method. It's not that Roussel's explanation is obscure or inadequate; for each of his words, it is absolutely efficient. Nor is it a question of there being something hidden; perhaps Roussel doesn't tell all, but neither is he hiding anything. The difficulty in this text, as in all the others, stems in some way from Roussel himself, in his extreme meticulousness and his severe brevity: a certain way of making language go through the most complicated course and simultaneously take the most direct path in such a way that the following paradox leaps out as evident: the most direct line is also the most perfect circle, which, in coming to a close, suddenly becomes straight, linear, and as economical as light. This effect is not on the order of style, but belongs to the relationship language bears to the ground it must cover. It is the formal organizing principle of the seventeen genesis-texts, in which the whole trajectory of the narrative and of time traces the entire instantaneous straight line that goes from a sentence to its marvelously identical, diametrical opposite.

The verbal wealth from which *Impressions d'Afrique* is drawn is therefore this: "*Les lettres du blanc sur les bandes du vieux billard.*" In order not to have to say it again (yet with Roussel it's always necessary to repeat), it must be noted that the word *lettres* (letters) is not used. It will reappear many times in the narrative in all its meanings, as one of the images or resources most often selected (for example, in the Rul, Massen, and Djizmé episodes). But it does not dictate the construction of the language, perhaps because that is what it designates, perhaps because the entire scenic structure is prescribed internally by the words both hidden and revealed there, just as the letters are visible signs— black on white, white on black—wherein dwell words that live and sleep beneath these strange signs. The whole of the *Impressions d'Afrique* is no more than letters (signs and cryptograms) written in the negative (in white), then brought back to the black words of a legible and common language. The word "letter" is not part of the game because it is being held in reserve to designate the novel in its entirety. I can't refrain from decoding this word as it applies to the title. This is an example of a negative form which, when applied to a surface and seen at a glance, leaves its own reversed image—the positive—in the same way that materials are "imprinted." It is this meaning that I believe can be read in the word *impressions,* which appears on the facade of the edifice. Obviously this is only a hypothesis, not that this reading of it is subjective; it is there in the autonomous meaning of the word. Perhaps Roussel did not foresee it. He knew, however, that language can never be disposed of absolutely. He plays with the subject that speaks, with his repetitions and his divisions. But let's go on to something more definite.

The eponymous sentence displays, in its two versions, a play of metagrams: *billard/pillard.* The first word is dropped and the second used, but not directly as itself. (I don't think that the word *pillard* [plunderer] is used once in the 455 pages of the text to designate Talou, a good man, after all, though jealous, ill-tempered, and given to disguises.) It will only be used through a haze of associations: cutoff heads, tawdry fineries, spoils, the old hereditary conflicts of former cannibal dynasties, punitive expeditions, hoarded treasures, sacked cities. From this fact can be derived a first principle: whereas the two homonymic sentences are what is most evident in the early works—exalted at the beginning and at the end of the narrative like the cryptographic bands on the cushions of the billiard table—they are now thrust back within the text, which, instead of being limited by them, functions as a thick envelope. In truth, they are not buried at the same depth: the antiword (*pillard*, plunderer) is visibly indicated even if it does not appear. It appears as a watermark beneath all the real words, readily visible against the light. What had been the final sentence thus rightfully remains on the verge of visibility and enunciation. In turn, the eponymous sentence falls outside the realm of any possible visibility (there is not the least appearance of a billiard table or a piece of chalk). However, it remains in fact the exacting organizer, since without it there would not have been any bellicose warriors, nor European captives, nor black troops, nor the white man Carmichael, etc. It seems that the horizontal axis of the genesis-texts has been swung around and now shows itself vertically, as if standing on its head: what had been seen of language and of time at the end of the narrative, as if through binoculars, had started from the initial sentence by the necessity of returning to it. It is this and this alone that is found in the *Impressions d'Afrique*. It's as if one were reading, linked together, all the final sentences of the early texts placed end-to-end in such a way that they overlay all the first sentences and the narrative distance that separated them. This causes a remarkable effect of liquid depth: by bringing the narrative back to the simple phrase that sums it up—"the hordes of the old plunderer"—it is possible to discern, as if at the bottom of a pool, the white pebble of that similar though imperceptible sentence; but it is only a surface undulation, a legible echo, and from within its silence, since it is never uttered, it sets free the whole brilliant and vibrant surface of words. So near, and so nearly identical, the nucleus sentence remains, however, at an infinite distance, at the other end of language where it is dormant and vigilant at the same time, watching over all the enunciated words, and asleep on its unsuspected reserve. It marks the limits of the gap that is opened up within the identity of language; it signifies the elimination of this distance. It is the mirroring effect of the unbridgeable space that has been suppressed, the space covered by the early texts between their identical boundaries.

This technique of a secret verticality could lead to no possible discourse if it weren't balanced by another, capable of opening a horizontal diffusion. Each word of the eponymous sentence is associated with a kindred realm: from billiard to billiard cue, which often bears as an inlay— a monogram of silver or mother-of-pearl—the initials of the purchaser, who during the game reserves for himself the exclusive use of it; which leads us to the word *chiffre* (initial/number). Each of these words will be treated as seminal words, used in an identical form but with a radically different meaning. The piece of chalk suggests the paper wrapping at its base to protect the fingers from the white dust; this paper is glued to the chalk, hence the word *colle* (glue/punishment), taken in the sense used by grammar school students: additional work inflicted as punishment. Only this second meaning appears in the text; the first, which is only a double, remains as buried as the billiard table at the beginning. The lateral extension, by way of association, is only made at the first level (billiard table, chalk, stick, paper, glue) and never at the level of homonyms, where the chieftain of the hordes or the punishment appears. Only the eponymous level is rich, continuous, fecund, susceptible to being fertilized; it weaves by itself the great spiderweb which stretches beneath the narrative. But if this deeper level has a natural coherence which is guaranteed by association, the second realm is composed of elements foreign to one another, since they have been retained only for their formal identity in relation to their doubles. These words are homonymous to the initial words, but heterogenous among themselves. They are discrete segments, without semantic communication, with no relationship other than a complicated zigzag that attaches them individually to the original core: detention (level 2) refers to the glue (level 1) on the white chalk (1) which produces the white man Carmichael (2); from this we descend further into white (1) which recalls the markings on the cushions (1); these cushions produce the hordes (2), where we plunge again toward the edges of the billiard table (1)—this billiard which gives birth to the savage plunderer (2), etc. It's a star-shaped structure which immediately indicates the task of the narrative: to discover a curve that will touch all the exterior points of the star, all the pointed verbal extremes which have been projected to the periphery by the dark explosion, now silenced and cold, of the first language.

Now the game consists of retracing the distance produced by the dispersion of a sentence reduced to its homonyms, independent of any coherent meaning. It's a matter of covering this distance as quickly as possible and with the least number of words, by tracing the only line that is adequate and necessary. Then, turning around its own motionless center, black and shining, this solar wheel will give language its regular motion and carry it to the light of a visible text—visible but not transparent, since nothing that upholds it will be decipherable any longer. And in the guise of a language that develops in freedom through whimsical material, ordered by a wandering, indolent, sinuous imagination, an enslaved language is doled out by the millimeter, cautious about the direction it takes, yet forced to cross an enormous distance because it is linked from inside to the simple, silent sentence which remains mute within it.

Between two points of the star a triangle is formed whose base is designated by the equivocal preposition *à*. The task is to project language from one point *to* another in a trajectory which will duplicate the natural affinity—masking it as it responds to its impulse—which links a piece of white chalk to *(à)* the glue of the paper wrapping it, a billiard cue to the initial of its owner, a bolt of old material to the darning which repairs the tear (a relationship which makes it possible to speak of *bande à reprises* [recovery band/pick up the darning strip], *queue à chiffre* [a monogrammed cue/initialed train] . . .). The preposition *à* seems to have two functions; or rather, the narrative is working toward bringing the *à* in the trajectory as close as possible to the possessive *à;* little by little the thread of language, starting from *blanc* (white), reaches *la colle* (the glue), and *blanc* by the same token becomes *"à colle"* (what distinguishes it from other characters is the additional element). With two words separated by a void, the machinery of language succeeds in creating a profound, substantial unity, more anchored, more solid, than any similarity of form. From the hollow opening inside words are fashioned beings endowed with strange characteristics, which seem to have been part of them since the beginning of time and forever inscribed in their destiny, yet are nothing more than the wake of the motion of words. In the early texts the repetition of language occurred in a rarefied state (reproduction, and inside this reproduction the statement of a void); now the language experiences the distance of repetition only as a place for the mute apparatus of a fantastical ontology. The scattering of words allows an improbable joining of beings. These nonbeings circulating inside the language are strange things, a dynasty of the improbable: *crachat à delta*

Rhyme and Reason

37

(delta of spittle), *boléro à remise* (cut-rate vest), *dragon à élan* (springing dragon), *martingale à Tripoli* (checkrein of Tripoli).

The gaps between the words are a never ending source of wealth. Leave the first domain of "billiard" and let other groups of words enter this magnetic field haphazardly; and as they appear, the mechanism of the process will treat them the same way: it will insert its blade into their girth and bring forth two strange meanings while maintaining the unity of form. These new eponymous couples sometimes have a sanctioned form *(maison à espagnolettes* [house with window bolts], *cercle à rayons* [sunburst], *vestes à brandebourgs* [jacket fastened with frogs], *roue à caoutchouc* [rubber wheel], *tulle à pois* [spotted tulle], *quinte à résolution* [a musical fifth in resolution]); but often they meet on pretty tenuous grounds. If Bedu the engineer has installed a loom on the river Tez that is driven like a water mill, it is the result of a previous association: ". . . *métier* [work/loom] *à aubes* [dawns/paddle wheel]. I thought of a profession which required getting up at the crack of dawn."

If Naïr gives Djizmé a gift of a braid decorated with "small pictures of the most varied subjects," rather like pendants on a lamp, it is because of the association of *natte* (a braid a woman makes of her hair) and *à cul* (to the posterior)—"I thought of a very long braid." Or else if one is lucky enough to think of a double figure such as the words *crachat* (spittle/grand decoration such as a star or cross) and *delta* (Greek letter/river delta), what comes to mind first? A decoration with a triangular shape similar to that of the Greek letter written in capital? Or a man sending a mighty, abundant stream of saliva so effluvial that it spreads like the Rhône or the Mekong into a delta? This is what Roussel thinks of first.

But I'm not following the rules. My opinion as to the appropriateness of these *"rencontres à tresor"* (meetings of gems) has no relevance. What we are seeking is pure form. What matters is the sovereign role of chance in the interstices of language, the way it is avoided exactly where it holds sway, celebrated instead of obscurely defeated.

It seems that chance triumphs on the surface of the narrative in those forms which rise naturally out of the depths of the impossible; in the singing mites, the truncated man who is a one-man band, the rooster that writes his name by spitting blood, Fogar's jellyfish, the gluttonous parasols. But these monstrosities without family or species are necessary associations; they obey mathematically the laws governing homonyms and the most exacting principles of order; they are inevitable. And if this is not recognized, it is only because they are part of the illusory, external surface of a dark imperative. But into the entrance of the labyrinth, an entrance unseen because it is located paradoxically at the center, true chance rushes ceaselessly. Words from anywhere, words with neither home nor hearth, shreds of sentences, the old collages of the ready-made language, recent couplings—an entire language whose only meaning is to submit to being raffled off and ordered according to its own fate is blindly given over to the grandiose decoration of the process. At the start no instrument or stratagem can predict their outcome. Then the marvelous mechanism takes over and transforms them, doubles their improbability by the game of homonyms, traces a "natural" link between them, and delivers them at last with meticulous care. The reader thinks he recognizes the wayward wanderings of the imagination where in fact there is only random language, methodically treated.

What I see there is not automatic writing as such but the most conscious writing of all: it has mastered all the imperceptible and fragmentary play of chance. It has sealed all the interstices of language where it could insidiously creep in. It has eliminated gaps and detours and exorcised the nonbeing which is activated when one speaks. It has organized a space that is full, solid, massive; where nothing can threaten the words as long as they remain obedient to their principle. It sets up a verbal world whose elements stand tightly packed together against the unforeseen: it has turned to stone a language which refuses sleep, dreams, surprise, *events* in general, and can hurl a fundamental challenge toward time. But this is accomplished by totally removing all that is random at the origin of everything that has speech, on that silent axis where the possibilities of language take shape. Chance does not speak essentially through words nor can it be seen in their convolution. It is the eruption of language, its sudden appearance: it's the reserve from which the words flow, this absolute distance of language from itself, which makes it speak. It's not a night atwinkle with stars, an illuminated sleep, nor a drowsy vigil. It is the very edge of consciousness. It shows that at the moment of speaking the words are already there, while before speaking there was nothing. Short of awakening, there is no consciousness. But at daybreak the night lies before us, shattered into obstinate fragments through which we must make our way.

The only serious element of chance in language does not occur in its internal encounters, but in those at the source. These occurrences, both within language and external to it, form its first limitation. This is demonstrated not by the fact that language is what it is, but that there is language at all. The process consists of purifying discourse of all the false coincidences of "inspiration," of fantasy, of the pen running on by itself, in order to confront the unbearable evidence that language comes to us from the depth of a perfectly clear night and is impossible to master. The element of chance in literary style, its biases and reversals, is suppressed in order to bring out the straight line of a providential emergence of language. One of the reasons why Roussel's works are created against the mainstream of literature is the attempt to organize, according to the least random discourse, the most inevitable chance occurrences.

The attempt is very often successful. The most dazzling must be cited since it has become, by being often quoted, Roussel's only classical passage. Here is the problem: "1st *baleine* (whale) *à îlot* (to small island); 2nd *baleine* (whalebone stays in a corset) *à ilote* (to Helot, a Spartan slave); 1st *duel* (duel/combat between two people) *à accolade* (to two adversaries reconciled after a duel and embracing each other on the field); 2nd *duel* (dual/tense of the Greek verb) *à accolade* (to typographical brackets); 1st *mou* (weak individual) *à raille* (I thought of a timid student railed by his fellows for his inadequacy); 2nd *mou* (calves' lights/lungs) *à rail* (to railway line)." And here is the solution: "The statue was black and seemed at first glance to be carved from one solid block; but little by little the eye could detect a great number of grooves cut in all directions and in general forming numerous parallel groupings. In reality the work was composed solely of innumerable whalebone corset stays, cut and bent to the needs of the modeling. Flat-headed nails, whose points no doubt must have been bent inward, joined together these supple staves which were juxtaposed with art, without leaving room for the slightest gap. . . . The feet of the statue rested on a very simple vehicle, whose platform base and four wheels were also made of black whalebone stays ingeniously fitted together. Two narrow rows of a raw, reddish, gelatinous substance which was in fact calves' lights were aligned on a dark wood surface, and by their shape, if not color, created the exact illusion of a section of railroad track; the four immobile wheels rested on these without disturbing them. A floor, adapted for carriage wheels, formed the top of a completely black pedestal whose front displayed a white inscription which read: 'The death of the Helot Saribskis.' Beneath, also in snow-white letters, could be seen this inscription, half French, half Greek, with a fine bracket: 'DUEL.' " So easy and so difficult is it, without any other throw of the dice than language, to abolish such a fundamental chance.

Ilote (Helot) is superimposed on *îlot* (small island). Simple phonetic displacement can build a whole medieval castle with crenellations and turrets from piles of coins (*tours en billon*, towers of copper coins); the construction will begin with *tourbillon* (whirlwind). "I decided to take a sentence at random from which I drew images by distorting it, as though I were taking them from the drawings of a rebus." For example: the folk song *"J'ai du bon tabac dans ma tabatière"* (I've got good tobacco in my tobacco pouch) gives *"Jade, tube, onde, aubade en mat à basse tierce"* (Jade, tube, water, mat object, to third bass). And Sapeur Camembert, instead of *"invraisemblable"* (unbelievable), used to say *"un nain vert sans barbe"* (a green dwarf without a beard).

"The process developed," Roussel said about this new technique, as if it acted without direction from him, like one of those simultaneously unforeseen, automatic, and spontaneously inventive movements made in front of La Billaudière, with him and without him, by his metal fighter: "Suddenly, the mechanical arm, rapidly executing several skillful feints, lunged in a straight thrust at Balbet who, despite his universally acknowledged prowess, wasn't able to parry this marvelous, faultless pass." This is a new aspect of the process: it's a blade thrust deep inside which strikes, against all expectation, the loyal adversary; that is to say, the reader, the language, or even Roussel himself, who is positioned in one location or another, behind the mechanism, to start it up, and in front of it to make the futile effort to parry its unassailable thrusts, its unexpected and deadly blade which by remarkable happenstance finds the opening, touches its goal, and majestically pierces it.

The originality of this seemingly natural "evolution" is extreme. The disintegration is greater than the one measured before, whose violence dislocated from their obvious meanings *"le blanc à retenue"* (the white man in detention) and *"la quinte à résolution"* (the musical fifth in resolution). It was then a case of separating the two sides of the same verbal surface. Now the physical entity of the word must yield up from its material substance elements of identity, like so many minuscule sequins which will be immediately plunged into another verbal body infinitely larger since it has to cover the volume of the secret explosion of words. Like a rocket from the fireworks shipped to Argentina by the cunning Luxo for the mad wedding of a millionaire baron, *"J'ai du bon tabac"* releases, in fragmenting itself, a completely magical oriental night: "The diaphanous image evoked an oriental landscape. Beneath the clear sky stretched a magnificent garden filled with seductive flowers. In the middle of a marble basin a jet of water in the outline of a gracious curve sprang from a jade tube. . . . Beneath the window near the marble basin stood a young man with curly hair. . . . He lifted the face of an inspired poet toward the couple and he sang a few elegies in his own fashion, using a megaphone of mat silver metal." *Jade* (jade) *tube* (tube), *onde* (water), *aubade en mat* (mat object).

The field of chance is no longer proportionate to anything known. Formerly the number of possible variations were those of the listings for the same word in a dictionary or in common usage. Thus it was always possible by this authority to discover the two words that are the inductor couple. The secret with which Roussel has burdened them is only a fact that can be suggested (for example, the incident of the sergeant major's sentencing the handsome Zouave, his rival, to a few days in jail no doubt occurred through the gap in a *"jalousie à crans"* (venetian blinds). But now the eponymous sentence is irretrievably lost. In order to discover it too many diverging paths have to be retraced, too many crossroads encountered: it has been pulverized. Over there lie words that are absolutely lost, words whose dust mixed with that of other words dances as particles in the sun. You may only know that it's a few verses of Victor Hugo (*"Eut reçu pour hochet la couronne de Rome"* [Had received for a teething ring the Crown of Rome] explodes into *Ursule, brochet, lac Huronne, drome* [Ursula, pike, Lake Huron, (hippo)drome]); the address of Roussel's shoemaker (Hellstern, 5 Place Vendôme, which evaporates to *helice, tourne, zinc, plat, se rend, dôme* [propeller, turn, zinc, flat, goes (becomes), dome]); the caption of a drawing by Caran d'Ache, the title of a novella by Barbey d'Aurevilly, fiery letters that shine from within the palace of Nebuchadnezzar (hence the incident of Fogar turning on the spotlight with a handle in his armpit). Roussel himself lost most of the other keys, and except by luck this first language cannot be recovered—its phonetic fragments sparkling, without our knowing where, displayed on the enchanted surface. The forms of dispersion authorized by a sentence such as *"J'ai du bon tabac"* (I've got good tobacco) are infinitely numerous; each syllable offers a new possibility: *geai* (jackdaw), *tue* (kill), *péan* (paean), *ta bacchante* (your bacchante); or even: *Jette, Ubu, honte à bas* (Ubu, cast down shame); or still: *J'aide une bonne abaque* (I help a good abacus). . . . It's easy to see that all these solutions are wanting in richness compared to Roussel's privileged creations; to go from familiar moonlight to the nights of Baghdad, a certain amount of calculated chance is required, and no doubt a certain direction mapped out under so many possible stars. The enormity of the risks that are encountered and overcome is reminiscent of the machine in the second chapter of *Locus Solus:* an aerial instrument for setting down tiny paving stones creates a mosaic of human teeth obtained by painless and expedient extraction; a complex mechanism enables it to fly from the piles of polychromatic incisors to the design, and, selecting the one needed, place it in the appropriate spot. The inventor has discovered the way to calculate in advance to the smallest detail the strength and direction of each breath of air. As with the multicolored syllables extracted by Roussel from the human mouth, a marvelous mechanism disposes of them by relying on the most hazardous and unpredictable movements. Everything about Canterel's machine is known except how he calculated the winds. Roussel's process is equally well known. But why this particular direction? How was the choice made? What current or what breath takes the severed syllable back to the language which rejoins it? Roussel said, not without wisdom: "Just as one can use rhymes to compose good or bad verse, so one can use this method to produce good or bad works."

Here's the original element of chance thrown back inside the work, not as a haphazard discovery but as countless possible ways of destroying and reconstructing words such as they occur. Chance is not a play of positive elements, it's an infinite opening, renewed at the very moment of annihilation. In this multiplication of the haphazard which is maintained and turned into ceaseless destruction, the birth and death of language is a continuum, giving birth to these motionless, repetitive, half-dead and half-alive figures, both objects and humans, that appear on Ejur's stage or in Martial Canterel's invention of a box for resurrection.

Brought back to self-destruction which is also risky birth, Roussel's haphazard language has a strange shape: like all literary language it's the annihilation of daily repetitions and it upholds itself indefinitely in the hieratic gesture of this murder; like daily language, it repeats incessantly, but the purpose of this repetition is not to gather and pass on; it maintains what it repeats in the drowning out of a silence that necessarily throws an inaudible echo. Right from the start of the game Roussel's language takes in what has already been said, which it embraces with the most haphazard element of chance, not to express in a better way what's already been said but to have the form undergo the second random fragmentation, and, from the scattered pieces, inert and shapeless, create the most incredible meanings by leaving them in place. Far from being a language that seeks to begin, it's the second form of words already spoken: it's everyday language ravaged by destruction and death. That's why it is essential that it refuse to be original. It does not attempt creation, but by going beyond destruction, it seeks the same language it has just massacred, finding it again identical and whole. By nature it is repetitive. Speaking for the first time of things never seen, machines never invented, monstrous plants, cripples Goya would never have dreamed of, crucified jellyfish, adolescents with sea-green blood, this language carefully hides that it says only what has already been spoken. However, he did reveal it at the last moment in his posthumous declaration; thus his voluntary death opened an internal dimension of language which was, after all, his own sentencing of that language to death and also its resurrection from the splendid particles that constitute its body. It's this sudden void created by death in everyday language, followed immediately by the appearance of stars, which marks the boundaries of poetry.

"It is essentially a poetic method," said Roussel. But formerly, with that placating reticence which determined the rhythm of all his behavior, he had both justified and diminished the scope of his declaration by explaining that "the process is, in short, related to rhyme. In both cases there is unforeseen creation due to phonetic combinations." If "rhyme" is given its most encompassing meaning, if it's understood to include all forms of repetition in language, then it's well within its scope that all of Roussel's work takes shape: from the playful rhymes which frame, in the manner of a refrain, the early texts, to the paired words of the first process which create the paradoxical echoes of words never uttered, to the syllable-sequins of the second process which point out to no one in particular the minute flashes of a silent explosion where this language, which is always speaking, dies. In this final form which determines the four major texts of Roussel's work (*Impressions d'Afrique, Locus Solus, L'Étoile au Front, La Poussière de Soleils*), the rhyme (modified into a faint and often only approximate resonance) just carries a trace of the repetition that was once louder, more charged with meaning and possibilities, more weighted with poetry. The language repeats itself beyond the enormous, meticulous mechanism that annihilates it, only to find itself formed again with the same materials, the same phonemes, and equivalent words and sentences. From the original prose of a language haphazardly discovered to the duplicate prose not yet articulated, there's a profound repetition. It is not the lateral one of things said again, but the radical one which has gone beyond nonbeing and, because it has come through this void, is poetry, even if on the level of style it remains the flattest of prose. Flat, Roussel's poetical Africa ("Despite the setting sun the heat remained overwhelming in this part of Africa near the equator, and each of us felt immobilized and ill by the stifling heat stirred by not a breeze"); flat, Canterel's enchanted retreat ("He is far enough from the bustle of Paris—and yet could reach the capital in a quarter of an hour when his research required a visit to such and such special library, or when the time came to present the scientific world, at extremely crowded lectures, with such sensational information"). But this flat language, this thin repetition of the most worn-out usages, is stretched flat on the enormous machinery of death and of resurrection, which simultaneously divides and rejoins it. It is poetic in its roots, as well as in its process of creation by this gigantic machinery which marks the points of indifference between the creation and the destruction, the dawn and the death.

4

Dawns, Mine, Crystal

THE THIRD PERFORMER at the gala of Incomparables, Bob Boucharessas, four years old, bears on his forehead the star of imitation: "With an astonishing mastery and a miraculously precocious talent, the charming tot began a routine of imitations executed with eloquent gestures: the various sounds of a train starting up, all the calls of barnyard animals, the grating of a saw on ashlar stone, the sudden popping of the cork of a bottle of champagne, the glug-glug of liquid being poured, the fanfare of a hunting horn, a violin solo, the plaintive melody of a cello—these formed a dazzling repertory able to create for anyone who would momentarily close his eyes the total illusion of reality."

The forms of imitation (of a duplication of things, of a return to the identical through action at the very moment of being copied) determine practically all the skills of the Incomparables (who are incomparable because of the ever-flattering comparison of their exploits with reality, result-

ing in a reproduction of it that is unique in its perfection)
and all the scenes set in the Solitary Place (unique apparently because of all the doubles flourishing along the winding of its paths). These marvels of duplication can take
many forms: men—or living beings—who, separating from
their own being, identify with other things to assume their
visible reality and to take on their appearance (Bob
Boucharessas or, in Canterel's liquid diamond, the ballerina who became an aquatic harp); things—or animals—
who, slipping away from their own domain and in obedi-
ence to some secret law, assume human action most alien to
any rules—or perhaps conforming strictly to the most complex of laws (Marius Boucharessas' cats who are athletes;
Mopsus, the rooster who writes by spitting blood; the invin-
cible metal swashbuckler); figures who imitate reproductions, taking away from them what they imitate in order to
reconstitute the original in some indefinable way. It is on a
higher level since it is about a redoubled splitting, but
elementary because this double imitation harks back to a
primary reality (the flying pile driver translates into human
teeth an old legend passed on for a long time by word of
mouth; the sea horses harnessed to their solidified sauternes bubble depict the old allegory of the rising sun).
There are scenes which imitate theatrical illusion, based on
them in order to extend them to the limits of the unreal (a
fake scene duplicates Romeo's last act with images fashioned from billows of multicolored smoke) or to reduce
them to the simple truth of the actor who is their double
agent (the obese ballerina reduced to the reality of an old
spinning top when the whiplash knocks her over; or what
constitutes the reverse image, such as the actor Lauze, restored to a semblance of life by the artifices of Canterel—
but only for that one scene where he reached the height of
perfection as an actor). Finally, there is the last or fifth
form, the indefinite imitation which reproduces itself, cre-

ating a monotonous line that triumphs over time (it is Canterel's double discovery of "resurrectine" and of "vitalium" which makes it possible to animate death with an endless repetition of life; it is also Fogar's tree: the molecules that compose its delicate fronds, brilliant and vibratory, are sensitive to such a degree that their organization and color reproduce exactly the space they occupy; they can thus register the images of a book—itself a record of often recounted legends—and reproduce them endlessly, even projecting them on the ground, so sharp is the picture, so fresh the colors, of this reflection of a reflection . . .).

Everything in these unique skills is secondhand, everything about these incomparable accomplishments is repetitious. The reason is that everything has always already begun; the incredible has already been heard and, beyond memory, the words have spoken from the depths of language. The wonder is that every renewed beginning starts from the unique, and reproduces it exactly, but duplicated and irreducible. The mechanism and the scenes already contain their final results, just as the words are hidden in the process whose function was to bring them to the surface.

These astonishing mechanisms for repetition in reality hide more than they reveal of what they have to reproduce. What is the meaning, in the first garden path of *Locus Solus*, of the black clay figure of a child, arms open in an enigmatic gesture of offering, and on whose base is indicated in a peremptory way that the subject is *"Fédéral à semen-contra"* (Federal wormwood)? And what is the meaning of the sculptured relief nearby depicting a "one-eyed man in pink clothing who . . . pointed out for several onlookers a medium-sized block of green-veined marble with an ingot of gold half buried in its upper surface and on it the word *Ego* and the sign for paragraph and date shallowly engraved"?

What treasure is silently pointed out here and there, only to be withdrawn the moment it is proffered? All these scenes are like spectacles, since they display what they show but do not disclose what is in them. They have a radiance in which nothing is visible, as in the diamond of mirroring liquid that Canterel has erected at the bottom of his terrace with a solar brilliance that attracts one's attention but dazzles too much for one to be able to see: "Two meters high and three wide, beneath the rays of the blazing sun the monstrous jewel, rounded in the shape of an ellipse, threw fiery beams that were almost unbearable, surrounding it with lightning flashing in all directions."

After the synchronic exhibition of these marvels, Roussel then proposes the secret story represented by their inter-play. This requires a "second navigation" around the objects, scenes, and machines, which are no longer treated as marvelous games in space, but become narratives crushed into a unique, fixed figure (with little temporal bearing) and indefinitely repeatable. The language of this second part of the text has the function of restoring meaning to signs, sequence to the simultaneous; and to reiteration it returns the unique event that it repeats. This second navigation is a voyage around a continent taken as a whole (in *Impressions d'Afrique*) or a coasting around each of the figures (in *Locus Solus*). Within this exposition, in these scenes of time regained, each element is repeated in its place with its meaning. For example, we learn that the one-eyed dwarf of the sculptured relief is a court jester, to whom the dying king confided a secret going far back to the remote history of the dynasty, which founded its power on a symbolic bar of pure gold. The narrative returns to the original moment when it started, recovers the image which stood at the beginning like a mute emblem, and now tells what it means. The combination of figure and narrative functions in the same way as formerly did the genesis-texts: the machines or the staging occupy the position of the isomorphic sentence whose strange images create a void toward which the language rushes; which even through an immense expanse of time leads back to it with meticulous care to form the *narrative time* of these mute forms. This time and this language repeat the eponymous figure since they explain it, return it to its first occurrence, and restore its actual stature. But it could just as well be said (and this is not the case with the genesis-texts) that the mechanism repeats the contents of the narrative, which it projects forward beyond time and beyond language, according to a system of translation which triumphs over duration as it does over words. The system is thus reversible: the narrative repeats the mechanism that creates the narrative.

As for the shift in meaning (essential and obvious in the isomorphic sentences), it is now hidden inside the mechanisms whose structure is secretly dictated by a series of eponymous words, repeated according to the laws of the process. Roussel's machines are thus bifurcated and doubly wonderful: they repeat in one language which is spoken and coherent, another which is mute, spent, and destroyed; they also repeat in fixed images without words the long sentence of a story: an orthogonal system of repetitions. They are situated exactly at the point where language is articulated, a point both dead and alive; they are the language which is born of suppressed language (consequently poetry); they are the figures which take form in language before discourse and before words (also poetry). Before and after that which is articulated, they are the language rhyming with itself: repeating from the past whatever still lives in the word (killing it by the simultaneously formed figure), repeating everything that is silent, dead, and secret in what is spoken (and making it live as a visible image). A rhyme becomes an echo at the ambiguous moment when language is at the same time the victim and the murderer, the resurrection and suppression of itself. There, language experiences a death that clings to life, and its very life is prolonged in death. At this point it is the repetition, the reflection in which death and life mirror each other, and each places the other in doubt. Roussel invented language machines that have no other secret outside of the process than the visible and profound relationship that all language maintains with, disengages itself from, takes up, and repeats indefinitely with death.

This is confirmed in an easily understood way by the main character of *Locus Solus;* in it Canterel explains a procedure in which one can't fail to recognize, not the process, but rather its relationship to the whole of Roussel's language: the process of the process. "Having experimented for a long time on cadavers placed under timely refrigeration and at the required temperature, the master, after much trial and error, finally made a discovery that used one part vitalium to one part resurrectine—a reddish matter in an erythritol base which, injected as a liquid through a laterally pierced opening into the skull of some deceased subject, solidified around the entire surface of the brain. The internal envelope thus created needed only to be brought into contact with the vitalium, a dark metal easily inserted as a short rod into the orifice of the injection, to cause these two elements, which are separately inert, to instantaneously discharge a powerful surge of electricity penetrating the brain and triumphing over the cadaver's rigor mortis to endow the subject with an astonishing factitious life." I will come back later to the restorative powers of these products. For now, I will only say this: Canterel's formula calls for *two* products, where one without the other remains inactive. The first, the color of blood, remains inside the corpse, covering the crumbly pulp of the brain with a hard shell. Rigid, it has the stiffness of a dead thing, but it preserves and maintains it in this death which it duplicates for eventual repetitions; it is not the rediscovery of life but death enveloped as death. As for the other, it comes from the outside and brings to the secret shell the vivacity of the moment: with it movement starts and the past returns; death is thawed back to time and time is repeated in death. Inserted between the skin and body like an invisible wax, or a solid void, the resurrectine functions in the same way repetitions, rhymes, assonance, and metagrams do between the surface language and the eponymous words: it's the invisible depth of Roussel's language which communicates vertically with its own *sustained destruction.*

The horizontal rod of vitalium, which introduces time, has the same function as the narrative language of the second level: it's the linear discourse of events which repeats itself, the slow speech curved to return. It seems as if Roussel before his death, in his last explanatory work where this form clearly is used, had always intended to revive it due to all these figures of the living dead, or more specifically, due to all these bodies floating in a neutral ether where time echoes around death as language does around its own destruction.

In their basic function Roussel's machines make all speech undergo a moment of annihilation, in order to rejoin the language divided from itself—and yet identical to itself—in so perfect an imitation that between that imitation and its model only the thin black blade of death has been able to penetrate. This is the essence of imitation (theatrical not just in its staging, but in its being) of all the "attractions" displayed on Ejur Square, or in the solitary garden. Little Bob Boucharessas' virtuosity is dominated by the same mortal division as the scenes played in Canterel's cold rooms; in one as in the other, life is repeated beyond its limits. The child imitated things that were dead; the dead doctored by Canterel imitate their own life: he reproduced "with a strict verisimilitude the slightest motions made during certain telling moments of life. . . . And the illusion of life was absolute: eye movements, the continual action of the lungs, speech, various gestures, the walk, nothing was lacking."

Thus the effects of duality never cease to multiply: the twice-repeated eponymous words (the first time in the scene with the machine or the display of skills, and the second time in the explanation of it or its historical commentary), the machines repeated in the second discourse according to the sequence of time. This narrative is itself repeated by the machine which, by making it immediate, reduplicates the past (often in an indefinite series) and divides the present by its exact imitation. It is a system which proliferates with rhymes, in which not only syllables are repeated but also words, the entire language, things, memory, the past, legends, life—each separated from and connected to itself by the fissure of death. What Roussel said must be heeded: "The process is in short related to rhyme. In both cases there is unforeseen creation due to phonetic combinations. It is essentially a poetic process." Poetry is the absolute division of language which restores it identically to itself, but on the other side of death; it is the rhymes of things and of time. From the faithful echo is born the pure invention of verse.

This is what is demonstrated on the plains of Ejur by Stéphane Alcott and his six sons. Six sons, all thin as skeletons, take up positions at specified distances from one another in a virtual architecture of sound; by constricting chest and stomach each forms the cavity of a parenthesis: "The father, cupping his hands to form a megaphone in the direction of the eldest, shouted his own name in a deep, resounding tone. Immediately, at irregular intervals, the four syllables, Stéphane Alcott, were successively repeated at six points of the enormous zigzag, without the partici-

pants having moved their lips in any way." Then going
from speech to song, Stéphane sent forth loud baritone
notes which, resonating to his satisfaction at different
points of the alignment, were followed by vocalizations,
trills, fragments of melodies, and happy popular tunes sung
in bits and pieces. (One seems to hear these fragments of
ready-made speech that Roussel's process undertakes to
echo in the density of his language.) By the marvelous
power of repetition hidden in the words, the bodies of men
are transformed into cathedrals of sound.

No doubt the most piercing echo is also the one that is
the least audible, the most obvious imitation, the one that
easily escapes attention.

All of Roussel's devices—the machines, the theatrical
figures, the historical reconstructions, the acrobatics, the
prestidigitation, the performing animals, and the artifice—
are, in a way that is more or less clear, not only a repetition
of hidden syllables, or just the elements of a story to be
discovered, but also an image of the process itself. It is an
image that is imperceptibly visible, perceived but not decipherable, revealed in a flash and without a possible reading, present in a radiance that blinds the reader. It is clear
that Roussel's machines are identifiable with the process, and yet
this clarity reveals nothing about itself; it can only offer to
the reader the silence of the blank page.

In order for the signs of the process to manifest themselves in this void, the posthumous text was needed, which
does not provide an explanation for the visible forms, but
brings to light what already was shown in them, crossing
the field of perception with impunity and blinding the
reader. The text published after his death (which at times
gives the impression of being the result of disappointed
expectation, and seems almost resentful that the reader
should not have seen what was *there)* was necessarily preordained by the creation of his machines and those fantasti-

cal scenes, since they could not be read without him and
Roussel never wanted to hide anything. Hence the initial
sentence of his revelation: "I *always* intended to explain
how I wrote certain of my books."

In *Impressions d'Afrique,* in *Locus Solus,* in all the texts using
the process, beneath the secret technique of language there
is another secret hidden, which, like it, is both visible and
invisible. It's the part essential to the whole mechanism of
the process, the weight that fatally moves the cogs and dials
—Roussel's death. In all these figures singing of infinite
repetitions, Roussel's unique and definitive act in Palermo
is inscribed as a future that was always present. All these
secret rhythms echoing one another in the corridors of the
work can be perceived as the metronomic progression of an
event whose promise and necessity is continually repeated.
In that way, all of Roussel's works (not only the last text)
contain a figure that combines the "secret" and the "posthumous": every line of it is separated from its truth—yet
manifest since it is *not hidden*—by this bond with his future
death which refers in turn to the posthumous revelation of
an already visible, already exposed secret; as if vision, in
order to see what there is to see, needed the reflecting
presence of death.

To reveal the process, which is not perceptible in its
invisibility but which radiates through all the figures of
Impressions d'Afrique and *Locus Solus,* is an immense task that
should be undertaken someday—but piece by piece, when
Roussel's works and their context are better understood.
By way of an example we have here just one machine
(Bedu's loom) and, in the general ceremony, the first char-
acters at the gala of Incomparables.

I would be surprised if anything in these festivities was
left to chance (except, of course, the introducing into the
system of inductor words). Of the nine chapters forming
the part "to be explained" from *Impressions d'Afrique,* let us

leave aside the first two and the last, which narrate the sentencing of the condemned and Montalescot's trial. From the third to the eighth chapters the peerless victims of the shipwreck each perform in turn the skills for their deliverance. Why does the zitherist worm appear in the same series with young Lady Fortune? Why the echo-men with the fireworks? Why does pathetic Adinolfa follow in the same procession the man who plays folk songs on his amputated tibia? Why this order and not another? The grouping of figures in series (indicated by the chapters) definitely has its meaning.

I believe that the first grouping (Chap. III) is identifiable as *the figures of chance mastered.* Mastered in the form of a duality (Fig. 1, two symmetrical jugglers [one is left-handed] form mirror images on either side of a curtain of balls that they throw back and forth to each other). Mastered according to the rules of a game (Fig. 2, a litter of kittens divided into two teams learns to play prisoner's base). Mastered by the duplication of imitation (Fig. 3, the child who presents a duplicate of the most unusual assortment of objects). But there is at the same time the inexhaustible wealth of chance (Fig. 4, the young girl disguised as the Goddess Fortune); yet as Roussel stated about the process: "Still, one needs to know how to use it." Thus Figure 5, the marksman who by firing his gun (Gras) separates the white from the yolk of an egg. However, chance is only vanquished by a discursive knowledge, a mechanism able to anticipate risk, outsmart and defeat it (Fig. 6, the metal swashbuckler who can anticipate the quickest feints and strike the final blow). This makes it possible, then, to attain with certainty a glory that is nonetheless dangerous (Fig. 7, the child carried off by an eagle as the result of his own cunning and the precious animal he sacrificed). This glory of chance vanquished is illustrated by three instruments: the first uses differences in temperature (Cf.

Canterel, the flying pile driver, the rule of the winds) to compose music; the second uses magnetized pencils to prospect for precious stones and metals; and the third uses the sudden leaps of a worm trained to execute melodies on a water clock (Figs. 8, 9, 10). This is also the first stage of the process: to accept instead of to suppress the chance element of language so that it is framed in its rhymes, to anticipate and build it, discover its treasures and its slightest flaws, and little by little to perfect the song. The undulations of the worm which by diving into a body of water frees this or that little droplet, which in falling sounds a recognizable note—is this not exactly the obscure selection of words in the flow of language, isolated, projected outside their original sound and pulsating with others, which becomes a magical instrument? From the duplicated figures of the jugglers, reflected as in a mirror and linked by the rapid trajectory of balls, to the worm from whom, one by one, the syllable-droplets of a polyphonic language fall away, the very direction of the process can be discovered exactly as it is defined in *How I Wrote Certain of My Books*— from "the white letters" to the breaking up of Hugo's verses into future pearls (his repulsive assimilation of earthworms to Hugo's rhyming lines was made by Roussel in his posthumous text, and we are familiar with Roussel's identification with Hugo which is the basis of his poem *Mon Âme*).

It seems to me that Chapter IV (second grouping) is *the song of duplicated language* (Carmichael as Talou's prompter, Fig. 11), of language repeating the story (the lecture in front of the portraits, Fig. 12) or things (demonstration of natural sciences, Fig. 13). This duplicated language has the strange power of splitting the speaking subject, making him maintain several discourses at once (Fig. 14, the torso-man and the orchestra; Fig. 15, Ludovic, the singer with many mouths). Thus it can be activated automatically—above and below the scope of reflection (Fig. 16, the speaking severed head; Fig. 17, the tibia flute); causing to speak what is incapable of speech (Fig. 18, the talkative horse; Fig. 19, the dominoes, cards, and coins whose simple spatial distribution, according to a chance arrangement, make an image the way eponymous words form a narrative); endowing human speech with a breadth and a power hitherto unknown (Fig. 20, the fantastic megaphone); and a capacity for a theatrical illusion where the imitation is identical to the life being imitated (Adinolfa, the great actress, weeps right into the wings "her limpid flowing tears," Fig. 21).

Should one see in the third grouping (Chap. V) the theater (Fig. 22) and its failure (the spinning-top ballerina and the whiplash, Fig. 23; Carmichael's lapses of memory, Fig. 24)? Is it the failure of these duplicates who are not in any sense understudies? I am not certain.

In any case, the song which follows celebrates the triumph of the process: the victory of rhyme, the creation of music (the polyphonic echo of the Alcott brothers, Fig. 25); the victory of the minuscule syllables developed by the process into a magical narrative (these are Fuxier's lozenges which, when dropped into water, expand into colored images, Fig. 28); the victory of words which, like fireworks sent up above the shadow of the process, illuminate the dark sky in a blossoming both symmetrical and the inverse of the previous figure (Luxo's fireworks, Fig. 27). In the midst of these machines of success, the blind Sirdah is cured: the scales fall from her eyes and she can see (Fig. 26).

Now I would like to pause at the image which directly follows this illumination, not because it is the secret revealed, but because of all the machines in *Impressions d'Afrique* and also, I believe, in *Locus Solus*, it is the one that shows the most dazzling isomorphism with the process.

The engineer Bedu has constructed on the shores of the

river Tez a loom (*métier à aubes*). (It silently suggests—as we know from the posthumous text—a labor that requires getting up early in the morning—Roussel's passion for hard work.) In the night its metal rods sparkle, illuminated by the circular eye of a beacon: against the darkness emerge "all the intricacies of the astonishing machine toward which all eyes converge," with Sirdah's restored eyes in the forefront. The ten pages of details would seem to be an exception to his law of brevity; ten pages on the workings of a machine which is, after all, banal, taken from the articles "Jacquard," "Loom," and "Weaving" of the seven-volume illustrated Larousse dictionary. These ten pages are without any surprises, except for two or three impossible mechanical details (these difficulties are resolved without any problem inside a mysterious box), which is the clue that the process has been introduced into the traditional machinery of weaving. Isn't this an intrusion in the usual structure of his writing? It is the river's current that generates the movements of the loom (as the flux of language with its coincidences, its elements of chance, ready-made phrases, and its confluences, indefinitely feeds the mechanism of the process). The paddles plunge into the water, sometimes in depth, sometimes skimming the surface, and their movements release, through a complicated system of threads which escape notice, the action of innumerable spindles whose spools wind rainbow-colored silk threads. The current of water causes the movement above it of other multicolored threads, distinct and nimble, whose interweaving will create the fabric. The play of threads is also a word play, in which appears through self-reference the shift in meaning which serves as the lead thread that will draw the ready-made sentences from the flow of language to the tightly woven and patterned work. Another innovation of the machine is that Roussel-Bedu has ascribed to the spontaneous motion of the shuttle box (finally working "by it-

self" for the first time since Aristotle) the functions that
Jacquard assigned to the arches, rods, and cartons: because
the shuttles function as inductor words. Following a hidden
"programming," the designated shuttle is ejected from its
socket, reaches the awaiting compartment, and returns to
its point of departure, leaving behind a transverse thread.
Thus in the process, preordained words spontaneously
leap out of their original sentences, cross the breadth of
language, and reach the other side—from whence they return in the other *direction,* their colored wake behind them
wound in its turn around the axis of the narrative. It must
be noted that the selection of shuttles is determined by the
paddles, but the movements of the paddles are dictated by
the requirements of the pattern of the design and the future
trajectories of the shuttles: it is the mysterious envelopment of time, a complex meshing of the automatic with the
willed, of chance with the finite, the blending of the *found*
with the *sought after,* whose union occurs inside this oblong,
forever-closed black box, yet whose purpose is "to activate
the whole," and which is suspended between stream and
fabric, between paddle and shuttle, between current and
thread. It is the brain of a machine for weaving, strangely
resembling a coffin. Is it death which is there, serving as a
relay midway between the stream and the design, between
time and the work? It cannot be known. In this machine
everything is set up to be seen (the woven image itself
appears *right side out,* just as the narrative resulting from the
process does not show its reverse side), except for this
black box which will remain forever closed.

The material displayed to the spectators depicts the story
of the Flood (the reverse image of the machine: the force of
water not controlled, the flux that overwhelms the world,
driving to the mountaintops the "wretched condemned,"
perhaps as the extraordinary dangers of language threaten
those who do not master them). The loom is the opposite

of this twilight destiny; it defines what it is by drawing the Ark—the vessel of reconciliation, the sovereignty of the process, the place where every being in the world can with its own kind find its parentage: "Rising calm and majestic on top of the waves appeared the regular and massive shape of Noah's Ark, adorned with tiny figures wandering in the midst of a large menagerie." The machine (a mute reproduction of the process) reproduces an image whose loaded symbol itself points out its resemblance to the process; what it shows the spectator in a mute but distinct image is what it essentially is: an ark on the waters. The circle is complete, as the great cycle of paddle wheels, dawns, mornings, and words is complete, each of which in turn plunges into the current of language and from it silently draws forth the spell of the narratives. "Their number, their graduated sizes, the way they plunged into the water, separately or together, briefly or for a longer period, provided an endless variety of combinations, favoring the realization of the boldest conceptions. One might have mistaken it for some silent musical instrument, striking chords or playing arpeggios, some simple, others extremely intricate, whose rhythm and harmony were constantly recurring. . . . The whole apparatus, remarkable both in its assembly and its lubrication, ran with a silent perfection which gave the impression of a true mechanical marvel." What then is this strange sound, so perfect as not to be heard, this muted harmony, these superimposed notes which no hearing could perceive? No doubt it is this sound that, at the depth of Roussel's language, causes the reverberation of what one does not succeed in hearing. No doubt it is something like the imperceptible visibility of the process whose rigorous mechanism forms the interstices of all those wonderful and impossible machines.

Fabricated from language, the machines are this act of fabrication; they originate within themselves; between their

tubes, their arms, their cogwheels, their metal constructions, they enclose the process in which they are contained.
They thus give the process a presence without perspective.
It is assigned a place outside of space since it serves as its
own location; its dwelling place is its surroundings, hidden
by its own visibility. It was only natural that these contorted
shapes and numerous mechanisms doing nothing gave rise
to the idea of an enigma, a cypher, a secret. Surrounding
this machinery and inside it, there is a persistent night
through which one senses that it is hidden. But this night is
a kind of sun without rays or space; its radiance is cut down
to fit these shapes, constituting their very being, and not
their opening to visibility: a self-sufficient and enclosed
sun.

In order for all this machinery to become intelligible, it
was not a code that was needed, but a stepping back which
opened the field of vision, removed these mute figures to a
horizon, and presented them in space. It was not necessary
to have something *additional* in order to understand them,
but something *subtracted,* an opening through which their
presence would swing back and forth and reappear on the
other side. They had to be presented in a replica identical
to themselves, yet one from which they were separate. The
rupture of death was needed. There is only one *key* and that
is the *threshold.*

These divided and identical machines reappear in the
posthumous text. By a strange reversibility the analysis of
the process has the same outline as the machines themselves. *How I Wrote Certain of My Books* is structured as an
explanation of the forms in *Impressions d'Afrique* or *Locus
Solus:* first, the mechanism whose principles and evolution
are described as though suspended between heaven and
earth—as a series of movements which function indepen-
dently, pulling the author into a logic of which he is the
occasion more than the subject ("The process evolved and

I was led to take any sentence . . ."). Then once again the process is explained within a successive, anecdotal time beginning with Roussel's birth and concluding with a return to the process in relation to which the author's life appears as having been determined by it and forming its context. Finally, Roussel confides to it the repetition of his own existence for posthumous glory—just as he returns to the machines for an indefinite duplication of the past in a flawless reproduction beyond time. "In concluding this work, I return to the painful reaction I felt in seeing my works come up against a hostile, almost complete lack of understanding . . . and for lack of anything better, I seek refuge in the hope that perhaps I will receive some posthumous attention where my books are concerned."

Thus Roussel's last book is the last of his machines—the machine which, containing and repeating within its mechanism all those he had formerly described and put in motion, makes evident the mechanism that invented them. But there is one objection: if the machines only reveal their marvelous ability to repeat by covering over the imperceptible words and sentences, is there not also in the posthumous text a hidden language which speaks of something other than what is said, pushing the revelation even further away? I believe the answer is yes and no. If *How I Wrote Certain of My Books* makes the process visible, it is in fact because it abuts right up against something else, in the same way that the mechanism of the loom could only operate before the spectators' eyes to the extent that it was sustained and contained by the rectangular black box. This "something else," this subsurface language, is visible and invisible in the "secret and posthumous" text. The secret is that it must be posthumous and that death within it plays the role of inductor words. That is the reason why after this machine, there can be no other. The language hidden in the revelation only reveals that beyond it there is no more language and what speaks quietly within it is already silence: death is the leveller in this last language which, opening at last the essential coffin of the loom, discovers within it only its demise.

The last display of skill in *Impressions d'Afrique* is that of Louise Montalescot. Whereas the others perform for their freedom, she alone risks death. Her only chance of *survival* is in her accomplishing a prodigious imitation of life. She chooses to give an exact duplication of the most complex, the most delicate of landscapes: dawn in the forest, which is also, after all, a *métier à aubes* (work at dawn). "On the ground large flowers, blue, yellow or scarlet, sparkled among the moss. In the distance through the tree trunks and branches the resplendent sky; at the bottom, a first horizontal strip of blood red faded to give way to a band of orange above, which turned light to bring forth a very bright golden yellow; next came a pale blue, a bare tint, and from its midst toward the right shone one last lingering star." Between the bloodred strip which reddened the horizon marking the earth's limit and the clear sky with its solitary star is the symbolic distance in which Louise Montalescot must accomplish her masterpiece. Naturally she succeeds, as she does in reproducing the whole group of people that came to observe her (Roussel also loved to imitate people around him): "The warmest congratulations were lavished on Louise, who was moved and radiant"; and when it is announced that she is saved, she learns of "the complete satisfaction of the Emperor, wonderstruck at the perfect manner in which the young woman had fulfilled all the conditions he had strictly imposed." But in the kingdom where Roussel alone lived, there was no emperor, no amazement, nor any mercy shown. And the perfect machine will repeat itself in death.

There is hardly any doubt that Roussel is a close relative

of all the inventors, acrobats, actors, and illusionists who
make up Talou's little prison colony, and a near relative
above all of the universal Martial who rules over the garden
in *Locus Solus*. He is the ever-watchful engineer of the repe-
tition-machines. But he is also the machines themselves.

This leads to a rereading of *Mon Âme* (My Soul), the poem
Roussel wrote at the age of seventeen (in 1894) and published soon after *La Doublure* under the altered title *"L'Âme
de Victor Hugo"* (The Soul of Victor Hugo): "My soul is a
strange root where fire and water struggle. . . ."

It is interesting to compare this precocious machine to a
later one where there is a similar unity composed of fire and
water. In Canterel's garden, at the end of a high terrace, a
gigantic glass bowl makes the wonderful mixture it contains
sparkle like a diamond: water in which each particle, due to
an inherent luminosity, glitters like mica in the sun. It is an
innate fusion of fluidity and brilliance, of the secretive and
of the illuminating, since from afar it is only perceived in
flashes that catch the eye but also avert it, while up close the
glance can penetrate it without difficulty as though it were
endowed with transparency. In this crystal furnace a microcosm of Roussel's inventions can be discovered: human
instrumentality, as in Faustine's musical hair; the tamed
animal nature of the racing sea horses; the mechanical resurrection of death with Danton's talkative head; scenes that
blossom like Japanese flowers; the element of endless survival in the *aqua micans;* and finally the image with which all
this apparatus symbolizes itself: the golden bubble of sauternes solidified into a sun.

The forge of the soul is a strange underground cavern
that remains open to the sky. Along with a whole group of
admirers Roussel leans over the edge of this gigantic well,
thus looking beneath himself and, at his feet, the open and
burning hollow of his own head—his brains:

Sur la profondeur de l'abîme
Mon corps se penche de nouveau
Léché par la flamme sublime
Qui s'élève de mon cerveau.

Over the depth of the abyss
My body leans again
Licked by the sublime flame
Arising from my brain.

From this head thus severed (as will be the heads of
Gaïzduh or Danton), from this brain open to the sky (as will
be Canterel's diamond) which nevertheless remains at his
feet, Roussel sees a whole language arise, liquid and in-
candescent, forged by untiring workers on the high ground
where opens the mouth of the mine. There the metal cools,
is given shape by skillful hands; metal becomes verse; and
the ferment starts to rhyme.

Avec les reflets sur leur face
Du foyer, jaune, rouge et vert
Ils saisissent à la surface
Les vers déjà formés un peu.

Péniblement chacun soulève
Le sien avec sa pince de fer
Et sur le bord du puits l'achève
En tapant dans un bruit d'enfer.

With the reflections on their faces
Of the furnace, yellow, red, and green
They take from the surface
The verses already somewhat formed.

Painfully each one lifts
His own with metal tongs
And on the edge of the well finishes it
By hammering in a hellish noise.

Paradoxically inspiration comes from below. In this current from the underneath of things, which liquefies solid ground, a language is revealed which comes before language: raised up to the level of work—to the workers who come and go like the shuttles between the threads of the chain—it is ready to solidify into a hard and memorable metal, the gold thread of a sanctified fabric. In the depths sleep the images to be born; calm, worldless landscapes:

> *Un beau soir qui s'apaise*
> *Sur un lac aux reflets grenat*
> *Un jeune couple sous l'ombrage*
> *Rougit au coucher du soleil.*

> A beautiful evening descends
> On a lake with garnet-red reflections
> In the shadows a young couple
> Blush in the setting sun.

Thus Faustine, the aquatic dancer, dreams at the bottom of the diamond: "A graceful and delicate young woman dressed in a flesh-colored swim suit stood on the bottom and, completely immersed, assumed many poses full of aesthetic charm, all the while gently shaking her head."

The forge of the soul needs fuel: coal, solid black fire, conveyed by boats from the most distant lands. From this comes a confusion of masts, wagons, sails, forges, chimneys, and sirens, of green waters and red and white metal. And the soul-furnace, voracious mouth and open belly, absorbs everything that is poured into it. Canterel, the sovereign engineer of the soul-crystal, has with calculated care deposited within this fresh, sparkling reservoir the Cartesian divers, the furless cat, Danton's peeled brain, the sauternes solar bubble, the upright harnessed teams of sea horses, and, not without difficulty, the frightened Faustine, not as nutrients to be ground down, but as flowers that will blossom.

The differences are obvious. The diamond in *Locus Solus* is completely aerial, as if suspended in midair; its luster is perfect—promising survival, but nevertheless disquieting: has not the coldness of death slipped into it, that coldness one will soon find again in the refrigerated morgue? At ground level, the first soul is stifling: coal, red metal, the thick smelting is cast in a menacing but abundant furnace; everything is weighty in these raw materials. Everything is weightless and clear in the crystal; the marvelous water (air and drink, the absolute nourishment) is a sort of transparent carbon, resolved, already without substances: pure flame, light gas, a diamond fluid as water. It is the motionless and inexhaustible driving force of a life which indeed does not have to be complete. What is thrown into it floats, or dances, or effortlessly follows the graceful alternation of rising and falling. Whoever drinks of it becomes slightly drunk. It is at the same time pure expansion and complete reserve. It tells of the enchantment of a place where certain figures come to flourish without effort or clamor, who enact silent movements, tirelessly repeated, in which the soul can find the repose of time.

The forge, on the contrary, was deafening: hammers, metal being struck, poking: "The noise of cannon which deafens." Canterel's crystal would be perfect silence if it was not enhanced, as though in excess, by a barely audible music which one could believe to be that of its interior glow. "Little by little, as one approached, one perceived faint music, wonderful in effect, consisting of a strange series of characteristic rising and descending arpeggios of the scale," as if the water itself was sonorous.

One has the impression that on emerging from the ground where it was originally buried, the heavy machinery of the mine, without changing the order of its parts in any way nor the direction of its mechanism, has now become earnest, light, transparent, and musical. The values have been reversed: coal has become shimmering water; the embers, crystal; the melting, freshness; the dark, light; noise, harmony. The confused work of the anthill has abated; henceforth all movements revolve without friction around an unseen axis—the great internal silent law. Haste and bustle have forever been lulled to sleep in the ceremony of repetitions. Earth has become ether. It is perhaps this change, or something of this order, that Roussel points to by his sentence: "At last, around thirty, I felt that I had found my path by those combinations of words I mentioned."

And then all these lovely aerial machines—there is the crystal, the paddles, the flying pile driver, the aerial drop of water, the eagle and the child, the palm frond with a memory, the fireworks, the luminous grapes, the smoke sculpture, the metallic prism, the balls of the twin jugglers, and so many others—which will land on solid ground according to their own cycle. There they will not find the fiery disorder of the mine, but a well-tended and frozen garden, like the one in which Canterel preserves his dead: this is the garden surveyed for a last time in *How I Wrote Certain of My Books*. And there, just as they are about to disappear, they will discover the possibility of a new ascension where they will become even more serious—machines of pure glory (since no one is more of a nonbeliever than Roussel), which will complete cycles that henceforth can no longer be counted. Roussel evokes this eternally repetitive machine, this forge which beyond death becomes winged crystal in the stanza he added after the death of Victor Hugo, this other self, to the poem *L'Autre Guitare* (The Other Guitar):

> *Comment, disaient-ils*
> *Nous sentant des ailes*
> *Quitter nos corps vils?*
> *—Mourez, disaient-elles.*

How, they asked,
Feeling our wings
Shall we quit our vile bodies?
—Die, they said.

They—they are the light, imperious machines, and in the center of all of them, the sovereign process which binds together within its blinding crystal, in its endless weaving, and in the depth of the mine, both fire and water, language and death.

5

The Metamorphosis and the Labyrinth

ROUSSEL'S MACHINES do not manufacture beings; they maintain things in their state of being. Their function is to make things remain as they are: safeguard the images, uphold the heritage and royalty, maintain the glories with their sunbursts, hide the treasures, record the confessions, suppress the declarations; in short, keep under glass (the way François-Jules Cordier's skulls are kept under glass domes or the butterfly belonging to the prefect's wife in *L'Étoile au Front*). But also—to insure this preservation beyond its limits—to make things happen, overcome obstacles, pass through reigns, throw open the prisons and divulge secrets, to reappear on the other side of the night, defeating memory in sleep, as was done by Jouël's famous gold ingot, whose memory crossed so many gates, silences, conspiracies, generations, numbers, becoming a message in the rattling head of a buffoon or the squeak of a pillow doll. All these machines open, within the protective enclosure, a space which is also that of marvelous communica-

tion. A passage which is an enclosure. Threshold and key.
The refrigerated rooms of *Locus Solus* carry out this function
with the greatest economy of means: to make life pass
through death by the sole (and very simple, it should be
noted) virtue of vitalium coupled with the no less effective
resurrectine, by throwing down the divider that separates
them. This is in order to maintain a semblance of life that
has the privilege of remaining unchanged for an unlimited
number of performances. Protected by the glass which enables them to be seen, sheltered by this transparent and
frozen parenthesis, life and death can communicate in order to remain one within the other, one in spite of the
other, what they are indefinitely.

This past which still remains, riddled by so many communications, is no doubt the breath of all the legends, which is
magically opened and closed by the same unique phrase,
the often-repeated "once upon a time." Roussel's narratives, produced by such a complicated machinery of language, appear with the simplicity of children's tales. In this
world, placed out of reach by the verbal ritual that begins it,
beings have a magical power to form allegiances between
one another, to bind one another, to exchange whispers, to
cross the distances and the metamorphoses, to become
others and to remain the same. "Once upon a time" reveals
the present and inaccessible heart of things, which will not
pass away because it remains in the distance, and in the
nearby dwelling of the past. The moment it is solemnly
announced from the beginning that the story is there, the
days and the things of "once upon a time," their unique
celebration, and the half-uttered promise that they will be
repeated every time—each time, the flight of language
crosses the boundary, reappearing on that other side which
is always the same. By this very function of maintaining
beings, Roussel's machines create tales of their own accord:
a form of the fantastic continuously kept within bounds by

the boxwood edging of the fable. Equivocably Roussel's tales can be read in two directions (Roussel advised uninitiated readers of *Impressions d'Afrique* to read the second part before the first), because it is the machines which produce the tales, and it is also the tales which remain within the machines. Leiris defined it wonderfully: "The products of Roussel's imagination are the commonplace made quintessential: as disconcerting and singular as he is for the public, in fact he drew from the same sources as popular imagination and children's imagination. No doubt the almost unanimous incomprehension which Roussel painfully encountered is due less to an inability to attain the universal than to this unusual alliance of the everyday commonplace and the quintessential." The process produces ready-mades, and immemorial narratives cause the birth of machines never before seen. This closed discourse, hermetically sealed by its repetitions, opens from within onto the oldest issues of the language and makes an architecture without a past suddenly rise. That's perhaps where his relationship to Jules Verne becomes apparent.

Roussel himself has stated how he admired him: "From certain pages of *Voyage to the Center of the Earth*, to *Five Weeks in a Balloon*, to *Twenty Thousand Leagues Under the Sea*, to *From the Earth to the Moon*, to *Circling the Moon*, to *The Mysterious Island*, to *Hector Servadac*, he rises to the highest attainment of human language. I had the happiness of visiting him once at Amiens, where I was stationed for my military service, and was able to shake the hand that wrote so many immortal works. O supreme Master, blessed are you for the sublime hours I have spent my whole life in reading and rereading you continuously." And to Michel Leiris' father he wrote in 1921: "Ask me to give up my life, but don't ask me to lend you Jules Verne. I am such a fanatic about his works that I am jealous of them. If you reread them, I beg of you never even to utter his name before me, for it seems to me that it's a sacrilege to pronounce his name other than while kneeling. He is by far the greatest literary genius of all time; his work will 'remain' when all the authors of our period will have been forgotten for a long time." In truth, few works can travel less, are more immobile than those of Raymond Roussel: nothing in them moves except for these internal motions predetermined by the enclosed space of the machines; nothing is out of place; everything sings of the perfection of a peace that vibrates within itself and whose every figure shifts position only to better indicate its place and immediately return to it. Nor is there in Roussel any sense of anticipation: invention opens no future; it is completely introverted, having no other role than to protect against the erosion of time a figure that it alone has the power to maintain in a technical eternity, barren and cold. The tubes, the threads, the magnetic propagations, the rays, the chemical effluvium, the nickel porticoes have not been positioned to determine a future but only to slide in the narrow space that separates the present from the past and thus to maintain the figures of time. That's why there's no question of ever using these instruments: the shipwreck of the Incomparables, all their attractions saved, their demonstration of them during a celebration are symbolic of the essentially gratuitous nature which is further underlined by the solitude of Canterel's garden. All these unknown instruments have no future other than their rehearsal of the performance and their return to being the same.

It is this being haunted by the return that's common to both Jules Verne and Raymond Roussel (the same attempt to eliminate time by the circular nature of space). They rediscovered in these unimaginable figures which they never stopped inventing the old myths of departure, of loss, and of return, those correlatives of the *same* which becomes *other* and of the *other* which was fundamentally the *same,* of the straight line to infinity which is identical to the circle.

The instruments, stage settings, performances, and skills exercise two great mythical functions for Roussel: those of joining and discovery. To join beings across the greatest distances of the cosmos (the earthworm and the musician, the rooster and the writer, the heart of a loaf of bread and marble, tarot cards and phosphorous); to join incompatible elements (the water line and the thread of material, chance and the rules, infirmity and virtuosity, puffs of smoke and the mass of a sculpture); to join beyond any conceivable dimension ranges of sizes without relation (scenes carved in grape seeds; musical mechanisms hidden in the thickness of tarot cards). But also to rediscover a vanished past (a lost final act of *Romeo and Juliet*), a treasure (that of Hello), the secret of a birth (Sirdah), the author of a crime (Rul or the soldier struck by a bolt from the red sun of Tsar Alexis), a lost formula (Vascody's metallic lace), a fortune (Roland de Mandebourg), or a reason (by a return of the past in the sudden cure of Seil-Kor or in the progressive one of Lucius Egroïzard). Most of the time to join and to rediscover are the two mythic aspects of one and the same figure. Canter-el's corpses treated with resurrectine join life and death by recreating the past exactly. Inside the great brilliant crystal where Roussel's dreams float, there are the figures which join (the tresses-harp, the cat-fish, the harnessed sea horses) and those which are discoveries (Danton's still-talkative head, the figures of divers going up and down preserving fragments of history or legend, the harness which recreates the chariot of the rising sun); and then between the one and the other a violent short circuit: a cat-fish electrifies Danton's brain to make him repeat his old speech. In these games imitation has a privileged place. It's the most efficient means by which joining is identified with discovery. Whatever imitates in fact crosses the world, the substance of beings, the hierarchy of species to arrive at the place of the original and rediscover in itself the truth of this other being. Louise Montalescot's machine with the tangle of its electric wires joins the great living forest to the genius of the painter by the automatic movement of the wheel; and in doing this she rediscovers the very thing in front of which she is standing. It's as if she had joined so many differences between them only to rediscover the identity of the duplicate.

Thus are constructed and crisscrossed the mechanical figures of the two great mythic spaces so often explored by Western imagination: space that is rigid and forbidden, surrounding the quest, the return, and the treasure (that's the geography of the Argonauts and of the labyrinth); and the other space—communicating, polymorphous, continuous, and irreversible—of the metamorphosis, that is to say, of the visible transformation of instantly crossed distances, of strange affinities, of symbolic replacements (the place of the human beast). But it must be remembered that it's the Minotaur who watches within Daedalus' palace, and after the long corridors, he is the last challenge; on the return journey, the palace which imprisons him, protects him, was built for him, manifests externally his mixed monstrous nature. On Ejur Square as in Canterel's garden, Roussel has erected minuscule labyrinths watched over by circus Minotaurs, but where it is a question of the fate and death of men. Michel Leiris once again said it: "By joining apparently gratuitous elements, which he himself was not wary of, he created real myths."

The metamorphosis, with all of its related figures, occurs in *Impressions d'Afrique* and *Locus Solus* according to a set number of rules which are evident. To my knowledge there is one sequence of metamorphoses in the category of magical spells: it's the story of Ursula, the Huron, and the villains of Lake Ontario, who are under a spell (it's a system of magical punishment which takes on the image of a symbolic moral value, and in which the sentence lasts until the moment of freedom, at the same time predetermined but uncertain). Aside from this episode, there are no mice transformed into coachmen, nor pumpkins becoming coaches. But rather, the juxtaposition within a single form of two orders of beings not close in the hierarchy which must cross a whole intermediary gamut in order to be joined. Skipping the animal kingdom, Fogar's palm tree is endowed with human memory; but the iridescent bird goes straight to the order of hard metallic objects: "The caudal apparatus was wonderfully developed into a sort of solid armature of cartilage which rose at first vertically to spread forward in its upper region, creating above the flight area a real horizontal dais. . . . Very sharp, the extreme back portion of the armor formed a solid, slightly curved blade parallel to the platform." Often several steps are eliminated, making the slow maturation of the metamorphosis into a vertical leap, a leap to the zenith like the metal swashbuckler whose blows cannot be parried, or a vertiginous fall into the darkest realms of being; when Fogar opens his veins, he draws from them a strange, soft greenish crystal: "The three blood clots that Fogar held side by side in his left hand resembled slender sticks of angelica, transparent and sticky. The young Negro had obtained the desired results by his voluntary catalepsy, whose sole aim was in fact to cause the partial condensation of his own blood needed to furnish the three solidified fragments so full of delicate colors." We have already seen men as disembodied as stone vaulting, ready to give out all the echoes of a cathedral. The old principle of the continuity of beings, which gave order in mythology to the confusion of metamorphosis and propagated it like waves of sap, now is replaced by a discontinuous vertical figure which hides even greater powers to disturb. These powers are all the greater because this separation from the hierarchic is at the same time evident and denied with strict simultaneity. Usually metamorphosis follows order and time; it is a passage. In Roussel the super-imposition of realms is hierarchic; there remains an immobile and definitively fixed gap in the general contour of the form that no evolution will come to resolve. The not-natural is presented with the Aristotelian calm of a nature whose being is drawn once and for all. The insects whose rings of light are carried through the signs of the tarot deck and glow on and off above the Maison-Dieu (House of God) do not come from a fantastic forest, nor from the hands of a magician; no spell endowed them with malevolent signals. Old Felicity found an exact description of the insect with a drawing of it in a treatise on entomology which she bought from her neighbor, the bookseller Bazin. Traditional metamorphosis takes place in a half-seen fusion, in the course of a long twilight; with Roussel the meeting of beings occurs in the broad daylight of a discontinuous nature, at the same time close to and separated from itself. It's as if they obeyed the principles of a telescopic ontology.

In Roussel's positive world the patience of the trainer has replaced the power of the magician. But nonetheless it is a sovereign power: Marius Boucharessas was awarded the grand order of the Incomparables *(le crachat à delta,* the delta of spittle) for having trained a litter of kittens to perform on the parallel bars. Skarioffski wears on his wrist a coral bracelet which is a giant earthworm that has learned to play the melodies of operettas on a water zither. But in this world of performance—the only theatrical results—the training equals the transmutation. Of course, long hours of patience are required and innumerable rehearsals; but the result is so perfect and the virtuosity of the animals has become so great that these marvelous skills come into play as if they were a profound essence. With a motion that is almost natural, the marine and solar horses set themselves free from the twisted bodies of sea horses, only to superimpose themselves on them, harnessed to the chariot of Apollo, which is henceforth pulled by these double and unique figures. The trainer is the mild, opinionated counterfeiter of nature who starts from a nature separated from itself and returned to itself as a superimposed image. (Isn't it the same way that the unity of language was divided in its volume by the process and maintained as duplicates in its unique text? Perhaps the separation of things and the distances of language present this unusual game. But this is the problem of the *Nouvelles Impressions d'Afrique*, not of the first impressions.)

And yet this synchronized and supple world is not a world of well-being. It's true that nothing there is cruel or constraining. Smiling Lelgouach plays refrains from Brittany on his amputated tibia. In playing the water zither the melodious worm has no recollection of his training: "He gave the impression of customary virtuosity which, following the impulse of the moment, had to play in a different way every time, a particularly ambiguous passage." The blood of the rooster Mopsus, and that of the dwarf Pizzighini, are only physiological oddities. Besides, what catastrophe could make these monsters dangerous by tearing them away from Canterel's garden or Talou's kingdom? What sudden violence could shake these strange animals, completely surrounded by the vigilant world where they have flourished? But this lack of danger and cruelty refers back to a darkness within the thing itself which is quietly contained there. Thus in the transparency of a crawling sponge shaking with hiccups, thirsting for blood, can be seen "in the middle of its nearly diaphanous tissue a real miniature heart," which, acting on a drop of water, projects a spray of precious stones. It's there within this heart common to man, to diamonds, and to the animal-plant that the terrible sun can be found. It's a heart which lives and is not alive, as in the fully expanded jellyfish, the musical tarot cards, and all the cold, animated dead. And its inseparable duality (frozen liquid, gentle violence, solid decomposition, and visible viscera) finds its powers multiplied and not lessened from being on the other side of the glass pane: it's a pure spectacle that nothing can interrupt or resolve, and which remains there, destined to be seen, displaying in broad daylight the internal being of its counternature. It's a persistent monstrosity, at the same time understandable and without remedy. This cruelty without claws (as in the rose, the peeled and naked Siamese cat in the diamond-bright water) radiates only toward its own center. It's probably this that can be called the horror: to an unsuspecting glance, the encounter with dead things which are laid open, a certain tortuousness of being, where open mouths do not cry out.

The old structure of legendary metamorphosis is reversed here. The satisfaction of rewards or consolations, the justice of punishment, the whole economy of retribution found in traditional narratives has disappeared in favor of a joining of beings which carries no lesson: the simple collision of things. The crippled character of legend, cured because of his resignation, becomes in Roussel's narrative a human torso who hurls himself at and bounces on musical instruments like a large amputated finger dancing on the keys of a piano. The child feeding the birds becomes here the cataleptic adolescent who gives his sea-green blood to mollusks (Snow White becomes Green Crystal); the animals who build a shelter for their benefactor become the crucified jellyfish who forms above his master's head a gigantic umbrella of twisting and turning arms. The people in the age of "once upon a time" could make animals talk; in Canterel's crystal floats "a human head composed solely of cerebral matter, muscle, and nerves"; this was Danton's head. A cat without fur swims around him and stimulates the dangling nerves by the means of an electric cone he wears as a mask; the muscles move, seeming to "turn in every direction the missing eyes"; what remains of the mouth opens, closes, twists, bringing forth in its mute fury long sentences silent as algae, which Canterel translates for his guests. This is an inverted metamorphosis, the cat-fish which makes the dead speak. From this head which has retained in its decomposition only the reverse of the mask (when it is masks which eternalize the dead), the language comes into being without voice and immediately dissolves in the silence of the water. It is the paradox of this mechanical reanimation of life, whereas the old metamorphoses had as the essential goal of their strategy the maintenance of life as alive.

That is the limit Roussel has deliberately set and traced around the marvels of his limitless invention. A rooster can be trained to write by spitting blood, or a rasher of lard can be made to sing in graduated measure (that is the rule of the art; cf. Jean Ferry); skulls reduced to a pulp can be made to declaim; the dead can be made to move; but to none of these can the combination of resurrectine and vitalium give back life. The whole order of animal life can be overcome, and mites imprisoned in a tarot card become musicians singing a Scotch chorus, but never does death become life again. The resurrectine demonstrates that resurrection is impossible: in this world beyond death that is staged, everything is like life, its exact image. But it is imperceptibly separated by a thin black layer, the lining. Life is repeated in death, it communicates with itself across that absolute event, but it can never be rejoined. It's the same as life, but it's not life itself. From the scene acted out behind the glass panes of *Locus Solus* to what is displayed in a flawless analogy, from the rehearsal to what is rehearsed, there's an impossible distance traversed by an arrow going from one word to the same word within the process, language extending its reign to find again the identical but never the identical meaning. Without a pause, repetition, language, and death direct this play where they join one another in order to show what they separate. Neither faith nor concern for the positivism of science has forbidden Roussel to cross the threshold of resurrection, but only the basic structure of his language and the experiment he performed on himself of ending (finality, termination, death) and of renewal (repetition, identity, endless cycle). All his machines function at the inferior limit of resurrection, on the threshold where they will never turn the key. They form the outward image of a discursive, mechanical, and absolutely powerless resurrection. The great leisure of *Locus Solus*, the "holiday," is an Easter Sunday which remained free. Look among the dead, Canterel said, for the one to be found there; here, in fact, he has not been resuscitated.

This special form of the duplication of life in death presents the exact reverse and symmetrical moment which is even nearer to the other side of the mirror: the moment when death erupts in life. Thus are reconstituted: the scene when the daughter of Lucius Egroïzard was trampled to death by fifteen bandits, fanciers of folk dancing; the last illness of the sensitive writer Claude Le Calvez; the second ending (according to a posthumous text rediscovered centuries later) of *Romeo and Juliet;* the great crisis that overwhelmed the groom with the red lantern and Ethelfleda Exley, the woman with mirror fingernails; the suicide of François-Charles Cordier when he finds out, thanks to runes carved into a skull and a small diamond plaque, that it was his father who killed his sister-fiancée. The aspect of life that is repeated in death is death itself; as if all these machines, these mirrors, these plays of light, these strings, these unknown chemicals extract from an evidently conjured death only its presence, and its dominion, which was already established. The scene plays death imitating life imitating death in a manner as vivid as it was lived in life. The barrier not abolished by the resurrectine repeats life in death, and in life what was already dead. And on an ordinary morning François-Charles Cordier will make the same gestures indefinitely: "His right hand searching in one of his pockets comes out holding a revolver, while the other promptly unbuttons his cardigan. Pressing the muzzle against his shirt over his heart, he pulls the trigger and is stunned by the noise of the shot which reverberates endlessly. We watch him fall down dead on his back." Without end and always beginning again.

In all ages, the aim of the metamorphosis was to have life triumph by joining beings or cheating death by passing from one state of being to another, but in Roussel's works it is transformation in symmetry, which is also its countermeaning: the passage of life to death.

The labyrinth is linked to the metamorphosis, but according to an equivocal plan: it leads, like Daedalus' palace, to the Minotaur, the monstrous fruition which is a marvel and also a trap. But the Minotaur, by his very being, opens a second labyrinth: the entrapment of man, beast, and the gods, a knot of appetites and mute thoughts. The winding of corridors is repeated, unless it is perhaps the same one; and the mixed being refers to the inextricable geometry which leads to him. The labyrinth is at the same time the truth and the nature of the Minotaur, that which encloses him externally and explains him from within. The labyrinth, while hiding, reveals; it burrows into these joined beings it hides, and it leads to the splendor of their origins. Thus the horror of Roussel's beasts without species is divided by the impossible and luminous trajectory of the labyrinth. The image of it is Fogar's acrobatics. Between a basket full of meowing kittens (those who in another scene performed on the parallel bars) and a carpet bristling with black darts where a moment ago a squid was writhing (twisting these same kittens in its tentacles), Fogar has lined up three ingots of gold bullion and prepares to throw a bar of soap in their direction: "The soap, appearing to execute a complete series of perilous leaps in a flying curve, then fell on the first ingot; from there it bounced by turning a cartwheel to a second gold ingot which it brushed for an instant; a third leap accompanied only by two very slow somersaults landed it on the third ingot of solid gold where it remained standing upright, balancing itself." Thus between two images of the world of animal metamorphoses, man's skillfulness (which earlier had been combined in a union twice monstrous) traces an improbable but essential line which miraculously stops at a designated treasure.

Roussel's labyrinths often lead to a nugget of pure gold, like the one Hello finds at the bottom of the green marble grotto. But this treasure is not wealth (the precious stones and metal found with the ingot only have the role of indicating profusion: a sign that the source had been found). If the old crown of the kings of Gloannic had been melted down, if the metal ingot had been hidden and the secret communicated to a one-eyed buffoon, and if there had been a magic iron grille and signs in the heavens, it was due to the necessity of both hiding and revealing Hello's birthright. The treasure is worth less in its function as an inheritance to be transmitted than as the keeper and revealer of origins. At the center of the labyrinth lies the birth, in eclipse, its origin separated from itself by the secrecy and returned back to itself by the discovery.

There are two types of beings in Roussel: those produced by the metamorphosis, duplicated in their being and standing in the middle of this opening, where there is no doubt the question of death; and those whose origin is beyond them, as if hidden by a black disk around which the labyrinth must turn in order to reveal it. For the first group there is no mystery about their birth; they emerged calmly from nature or from a schooling just as serene; but they dazzle by their expanded being. The others are ordinary men and women (their description is that of children's tales: simple individualized beings, all good or bad, identified the moment they come into play by established categories); but it's their origin which is barred by a black line— hidden because it's too remarkable, or remarkable because it's shameful. The labyrinth wends its way toward this glimmering light.

Impressions d'Afrique presents on the stage of the Incomparables many lovely metamorphoses leading through a maze of anecdotes which make up the light dramatic structure. Rul, the wife of King Talou, has brought into the world an ugly baby whose eyes are horribly crossed, and who bears in addition a red mark on the forehead (it is the *louche à envie* [cross-eyed with envy] and prefigures *L'Étoile au Front* [Star on the Forehead]). She abandons her baby in the forest, making everyone believe it has died, but the little girl is found, recognized by her eyes and the mark on her forehead. In order to assure the royal inheritance of her bastards, Rul—an unfaithful wife (she is also "cross-eyed with envy")—blinds her child. A faithless minister intervenes, and a mosquito hunter, a false mistress, a whole interplay of snares and traps, coded letters, a riddle, a suede glove with chalk markings, a bowler hat—and by the end everything is discovered; that is to say, Sirdah recovers her birthright and her sight. This story has repercussions beyond itself, in accordance with a series of frameworks that is characteristic of Roussel's labyrinths, in another sequence which both envelops and determines it: Sirdah's adventure is only the last episode of a dynastic feud begun when the twin wives of the founder gave birth to identical boys at the same moment. The tribunal on birthrights was embarrassed and silenced by such a marvelous duplication:

How to determine who was first? What is the absolute moment of birth? Whereas the metamorphoses are displayed without secret in the performance, birth is always seen as helpless or obscured. Sirdah's cross-eyed glance (she sees double just as her ancestor saw double on the fatal day of the births) which caused her to lose her birthright and later enabled her to regain it; the loss of her sight once her birthright had been regained; her blindness, cured on the day her persecutors are executed, indicate this interplay of eclipse between "birth" and "vision." In *Impressions d'Afrique* the pure spectacle of the Incomparables, a place of peaceful metamorphosis, alternates with the episodes of the labyrinth of birth, up until the central episode of Sirdah's cure and the exact relation of the enigma of her birth to the sovereignty of sight. Perhaps this is the essence of the celebration, of the festival in general: for once, to see a being completely, and in seeing it, to recognize its birth.

But why should birth be in eclipse and so difficult to perceive when so many monsters display themselves without any reticence? Generally it is designated by the sign of duality: the enigma of twin births (Souann's two wives; the simultaneous birth of their sons; the disappearance of the twin sisters claimed for a human sacrifice in *L'Étoile au Front);* the shame of hidden illegitimate births and parallel family branches (Rul's children; the disinherited nephew of the prefect's wife); identical and substituted children (Andrée Aparicio replacing Lydia Cordier in her father's affections); the boy and girl of the same age brought up together who are separated and united by love (Seil-Kor and Nina; Andrée and François Cordier); the rivalry between two branches of a family fighting over an inheritance (Talou and Yaour; and above all the treasure hunt in *La Poussière de Soleils*). In these dualities the marks of birth are blurred; the natural order is strangely reversed. It is no longer the parents who are at the origin of the individual, who bring him forth into the light of day, but birth itself which releases a duplication in which it loses itself. That is the beginning of a labyrinth where birth is at the same time prisoner and protected, revealed and hidden.

The double progression hides the relationship, but also facilitates the discovery of the single thread. The secret of the treasure, which would inform Hello of his birthright, was confided by the dying king to his laughable double the buffoon; then to a duplicate of this double, a pillow doll. To safeguard his son from the bandits who made him their prisoner, Gérard Lauwerys has substituted a plaster statue for him; to find his dead daughter, once again, Lucius Egroïzard tries to recreate the voice she would have developed had she been able to grow up. The birth that is hidden because of its dual nature is enclosed in a labyrinth of duality which finally permits its revelation. At the end stands revealed absolute identity—"Ego" inscribed in Hello's gold ingot, the unique treasure hidden and shown by the wisdom of Guillaume Blache.

This triumphant identity, however, does not reabsorb all the doubles in which it momentarily lost itself. It leaves behind, as its black envelope, the whole series of crimes tied to the process of duplication that must now be punished. Whereas the metamorphosis and training occurred in a unified world where it was only a question of being, the births belong to a divided universe, where good and evil, the just and the criminal, rewards and punishments are endlessly discussed. And the rediscovered origin, in order to return to its luminous state, necessitates the abolition of evil. That is why there isn't any cruel monster in Roussel, nor in turn is there a celebration without the aspect of punishment. And the severity of the punishment consists of the pure and simple duplication of the labyrinth constructed out of cruelty to hide the birth. Rul, the evil queen, blinded her daughter, so her heart was pierced by the insertion of a needle through the eyelet of her bodice. Mossem, her lover, forged the false death certificate of Sirdah; thus it is engraved on the soles of his feet with red-hot irons. Naïr, the ingenious inventor of a series of traps, is condemned to make them indefinitely and reproduce to the end of his days these tenuous labyrinths of threads, such as the ones he formerly made to help his accomplices. Thus the maze where the birth is hidden is reduplicated: the first time it is reproduced in order to be understood and unraveled; the second time it is cruelly repeated in public to punish the guilty. The origin is finally restored to its unity only by the triumph of vision; that is what separates the truth from its mask, divides good from evil, separates being from appearance (Tsar Alexis' solar red stare unmasks Pletchaïeff's assassin, who, transfixed by the bloody lens, is struck down by the same symptoms as his victim and dies of the same wounds).

But when finally brought to light, the birth was not simple. It was already foretold by a sign which anticipated the event. That is probably the meaning of *L'Étoile au Front:* the three acts of the play are taken up by a presentation of objects more or less banal in appearance that hide the secret of a birth. The labyrinth of their marvelous story as shown by Tréze, or Mr. Joussac, invariably reveals a remarkable origin linked to the birth of a child, to ill-fated or guilty love, to rivalries among descendents, to the conflicts between the legitimate and illegitimate branches of a family: hence the secret hidden and then revealed by these enigmatic objects. But before the inventory of this little museum is given, several negligible scenes indicate their meaning and perhaps their origin. It concerns twin sisters born in India, ordained by a heavenly sign as principal victims of a human sacrifice. It's this birthmark which is the subject of the whole play, a dazzling sign, however secret, visible and occult; each object of the little theatrical museum is imbued with it, and it was already shining at the portico: the star on the forehead. That is why the play concludes as it had begun and as it pursued its subject: by evoking the sign, the enormous element of chance and its evidence: "How many failed careers, splendid in the eyes of the ordinary, accomplish their journeys by sailing against the wind! Here one of our elect, misunderstood by his peers who fight against him through hunger, endures misery to attain his goal; where another would have lived in idleness, he gives to the world a strange example of assiduous labor and manly perseverance." Of course, here we are saluting Roussel in person. But above all, this figure we already know is joined to chance (notice "how curiously up and down the social ladder in all ages stars were bestowed on foreheads") and to repetition, since once the sign is manifested, time has preceded itself, the birth is already designated by disaster or glory, and history is no more than this sign endlessly repeated.

At the core of the labyrinth finally unraveled, the birth designated by a star on the forehead is shown for what it is: an image of metamorphosis where chance and repetition are united. The destiny of the sign, already cast, initiates a sequence of time and space in which each figure will echo it, will faithfully reiterate it, and will bring it back to the starting point. In all its swarms of adventure, life will never be more than the duplication of its star; its existence maintains what it was given before coming into being. The enigma of birth has the same significance as the scenes of life prolonged by the resurrectine: to show in one way or another the basic event (birth and death) in an exact repetition; for the one, the imminence of death, for the other, the promise of predestination, which is what life repeats without fail. At the most enigmatic moment, when all paths stop and when one is at the point of being lost, or at the absolute beginning, when one is on the threshold of something else, the labyrinth suddenly again offers the *same:* its last puzzle, the trap hidden in the center—it is a mirror behind which the identical is located. This mirror teaches that life before coming alive was already the same, as it will be the same in the immobility of death. The mirror which reflects the birth that's explained by the labyrinth is the one where death looks upon itself, in turn reflected by it. And the nature of the labyrinth comes infinitely close to the metamorphosis resulting in the passage from life to death, and in the maintenance of life in death. The labyrinth leads to a Minotaur which is a mirror, a mirror of birth and of death, the deep and inaccessible point of all metamorphoses.

There the differences converge and again take on their identity: the chance element of death and that of origin, divided by the slender sheet of mirror, is placed in the dizzying position of being the double. No doubt this is the same position occupied by the process when, beginning with the chance element of language, which it duplicates, it causes through metamorphosis a treasure of differences to spring forth whose identity it recovers by joining them in a labyrinth of words. The rule of the process is still to be read in all these duplicated monsters, in all these hidden births.

Perhaps the first character in the *Impressions d'Afrique,* Naïr, the man with the traps, riveted to his platform and condemned till the end of time to make imperceptible labyrinths of thread which are metamorphosed fruits (fruit-animal since they resemble a chrysalis in the making)—could this be the presence of Roussel himself on the threshold of his work, tied to it, unveiling it before it has come to term (by the radiating web spun by his minute spiders), duplicating his own end (by this unceasing torture), showing what it is through the depths of his language: a metamorphosis-labyrinth? "A prisoner on his pedestal, Naïr had his right foot held down by a thick rope lacing which formed a snare tightly fixed to the solid platform; similar to a living statue, he made slow, punctuating gestures while rapidly murmuring a series of words he had learned by heart. In front of him, on a specially shaped stand, a fragile pyramid made of three pieces of bark fastened together held his whole attention; the base, turned in his direction but sensibly raised, served as a loom; on an extension of the stand, he found within reach a supply of fruit husks covered on the outside with a gray vegetable substance reminiscent of the cocoons of larvae ready to transform themselves into chrysalises. By using two fingers to pinch a fragment of these delicate envelopes and by slowly bringing back his hand, the young man created an extendable tie similar to the gossamer threads which during the season of renewal spread through the wood; he used these imperceptible filaments to compose a magical work, subtle and complex, for his two hands worked with unequaled agility, knotting, tangling in every way the ligaments of dreams which gracefully amalgamated."

In the *Impressions d'Afrique* the metamorphosis provides the important scenes, which are linked together solely by the slight network of the labyrinth. *Locus Solus* is organized according to another scheme of checks and balances: in the maze of paths, impossible forms come forward; but in the cells for resurrection (that is to say, in the places of metamorphosis) difficult labyrinths are revealed (long tales of unusual births, treasures lost and found). In Roussel's plays, the balance is again disturbed but in another direction: the labyrinth carries it away.

But there is a crossover which is stranger yet. The figures of the metamorphosis appear in a sort of quasi-theater: the stage of the Incomparables, the coronation festivities, Canterel's garden arranged like a pastoral setting, marionettes of dead people. The vocation of all these strange mixed beings, whether from the depth of their nature or from the first day of their apprenticeship, was to be *seen;*

their skills were meaningful only for one performance. By contrast, the labyrinth, which only unfolds within a hidden landscape, reveals nothing that can be seen: it partakes of the order of enigma, not of the theater. Yet it is the structure of the labyrinth which completely upholds Roussel's plays, as if it were a matter of eliminating everything that goes into its theatricality, to let appear as visible on stage only the shadow play of the secret. By contrast, never is it more a question of masks, disguises, scenes, actors, and spectacles than in the nontheatrical texts: the metamorphoses are only brought forth on stage through a narration, therefore changed and caught in the labyrinth of a discourse given second- or thirdhand (for example, the imitation of Shakespeare in a scene added within a continuous narrative).

Roussel's work seems to have revolved completely around this relationship—including the texts which do not use the process. *La Doublure* and its cavalcade of masks, *La Vue* with the gigantic flower growing inside a glass lens, are of the order of metamorphosis, of vision, and of the theater. The *Nouvelles Impressions d'Afrique* pushes the spoken and invisible labyrinth of birth and parentage to the ultimate point of destruction of language. Perhaps the process is only a singular figure taken in a larger context where the labyrinth (the line to infinity, the other, the lost) and the metamorphosis (the circle, the return to the same, the triumph of the identical) cross each other. Perhaps the dimension of ageless myth is that of all language—of language moving toward infinity in the labyrinth of things, but whose marvelous and essential poverty forces it back upon itself by giving it the power of metamorphosis; to say other things with the same words, to give to the same words another meaning.

6
The Surface of Things

WHAT OF Roussel's books which are not included among "certain of his books"? Those questionable texts about which he said and repeated that they are "completely outside of the process"? Is their resemblance to those within it only due to a coincidence—not due to birth or to deliberate artifice? In 1928, while researching the network of communications beneath Roussel's language to show its absolute control, Vitrac had compared the clumsy actor whose sword would not fit into its scabbard in the first lines of *La Doublure* with the understudy in *Chiquenaude,* who plays the role of Mephistopheles, defeated due to the darning of his pants. To which Roussel answered firmly: "You must not look for relationships; there are none." There is no answering this. The moth-eaten cushion of the billiard table gave rise to Talou's initialed royal cloak (because the process is there as well as here). The worms and moths that devoured the red lining of the pants are not those mentioned by the understudy (because there is no process). It is a simple criterion. The fortress of the process must be left in isolation just as Roussel defined the subject and drew the exact boundaries at the moment of his death.

It seems that Roussel thought his early works were of no importance. But now we know very well through a whole body of contemporary literature that the language of *La Doublure* and *La Vue*, like certain useless spaces discovered by geometry, has suddenly become populated with literary beings which would be inconceivable without him. Neglected for a long time, today he is the foundation of a whole concrete world for which he blindly formulated the premises and axioms. In addition, one could prove that he is like the fundamental geometry of the process (which I will try to demonstrate). This language will appear as the place of prodigious births—and of many others still unknown to us.

After the failure of *La Doublure* (1897) and the resulting crisis began the whole "period of prospecting," which lasted from 1898 to 1900 or even 1902. No doubt it was the period when he was writing the genesis-texts (cyclical tales between repeated sentences), none of which satisfied Roussel except for *Chiquenaude*, published in 1900. We know that this was the origin of the process: the circular form is still used in *Nanon* and *Une Page de Folklore Breton*, which appear seven years later in the newspaper *Gaulois du Dimanche*. Soon after, the process becomes generalized with *Impressions d'Afrique*. Between the period of *Chiquenaude* and the period of *Impressions*, five texts appeared, all outside of the process. It is undeniable that *L'Inconsolable* and *Les Têtes de Carton* could have been written earlier, at the time of *La Doublure*, from which they are like falling stars. But *La Vue*, *La Source* (The Source), and *Le Concert* (The Concert) were no doubt written when the machine for repetition was already functioning. Since nothing ever authorizes doubting Roussel's words (he was too economical with them), it must be admitted that these three texts open within the realm of the process a parenthesis that delineates a rounded autonomous space, like a lens containing a minute landscape whose dimensions are not reducible to its setting.

As to the last work, the *Nouvelles Impressions d'Afrique*, completed in 1928, it was begun in 1915, right after *Locus Solus*. Only the writing of *La Poussière de Soleils* and of *L'Étoile au Front* interrupted it, renewing for a while the process which *Nouvelles Impressions* escaped. Thus the technique of repeated words only had exclusive hold during a fairly short period of time, perhaps less than ten years. It was during this time that Roussel gave up poetry (since the internal and inaudible echo of words between the clicking of Ejur's machine and the murmurs of Canterel's garden creates enough rhymes and alone defined the fertile area of the poetic foundation). But from the beginning to the end of his work, and without exception, Roussel's language has always been double, now holding discourses without the process, now holding discourses with the process. The first was in poetry, the second in prose. It's as if this fundamental poetics which almost exclusively preoccupied Roussel's life was duplicated by versification (*La Doublure, La Vue, Nouvelles Impressions d'Afrique*) and by the process (*Impressions d'Afrique, Locus Solus,* and the plays), with complicated interferences at times—interruptions, crossovers, and certain effects of duplication like the mixture of rhyme and of the process found in *Une Page de Folklore Breton* and also in *Chiquenaude*. Only one possibility is excluded: a language without either process or rhyme, that is, without duplication.

This double language superimposed on itself recalls the counterpoint that is constant in *Locus Solus*, which is heard beneath the visible discourse of the dead, Canterel's low voice explaining in prose what poetic repetition is being accomplished on the other side of the glass pane, and what rhyme is made to echo between life and death. Ludovic is also recalled, the singer with the enormous throat and multiple voice, who comes on the stage of the Incomparables to make batteries of harmonic canons with his throat: "With a pretty tenor key, Ludovic slowly began the famous *'Frère Jacques'*; but while the extreme left of his mouth was in motion, pronouncing the well-known words, the rest of the enormous pit remained motionless and closed. The moment when the first notes of the words *'Dormez-vous'* resounded a third higher, a second division of the mouth began *'Frère Jacques,'* starting from the tonic; through years of working at it Ludovic had succeeded in dividing his lips and tongue into independent parts and could without trouble articulate at the same time several linked parts of different tunes and words; actually the left side moved completely, showing teeth without causing the right side to move, which remained closed and imperturbable." One can entertain the thought that Roussel also learned to make his tongue forked and his voice a fugue, to superimpose his language and to silence for a measure half of his discourse (which is what he did by maintaining in silence the counter sentences of *Impressions* and *Locus Solus* up until the appearance of that other voice in *How I Wrote Certain of My Books*), while his writing, his unique mouth, gave the impression of being absolutely linear. This was an immoderate amount of work as was Ludovic's, who, "exhausted by the terrible mental effort, left wiping his brow."

It is reminiscent of Guillaume Blache's system of double entrances (a dangerous trick, as history has proven) on the threshold of *La Poussière de Soleils*. In order to put one's hand on the skull with the sonnets, which leads straight to a well hiding millions—a first glimmer of particles of the sun—one must push two doors, one as open as the other (so afraid was old Guillaume that his treasure would not be found), one as closed as the other (so frightened was he that it would be lost from such easy access). Once these thresholds are crossed, the path is the same; the two rival groups progress along identical stages. Perhaps also leading to the final treasure of the work—to this well, at the same time a mine and a forge, whose glow was shown from the beginning by the poem *L'Âme*—there are two roads which are the same, two thresholds for the same road, two doors that can be opened with one motion, the first being the secret (unveiled, thus becoming nonsecret) and the second being the nonsecret (because it does not need to be uncovered, remaining in the shadow and under the seal of a paradoxical secret). The absolute exclusion of one by the other is only the threshold of their identity: here on the one hand is the secret of the nonsecret and on the other hand the nonsecret of the secret. The key which locks and prevents all transgressions opens in depth a threshold similar as a twin to the one of identity.

Such is the ambiguity (by definition impossible to explain) where the portion of the work that is not revealed vacillates endlessly: it's useless to consider the additional burden of an occult process, of a secret that remains secret. That portion Roussel always placed outside of the process. This evidently does not mean that it was structured *without* a process; nothing prevents a strictly logical attempt to uncover *another* process in the texts that he did not explain, the only condition being that it not be the *same* process. Jean Ferry tried, without being absolute about the hypothesis, the Morse code for *Nouvelles Impressions*. Why not? I don't know whether it's true or false; I only fear—with all respect due such an ardent interpreter—that it is not good methodology. Before establishing the equation Absence of One Process = Presence of Another, it must be kept in mind that this absence could *also* be equivalent to the nonexistence of any process. It's necessary in order to open up the whole field of possibility only to consider that the

"other" works fall outside of the revelation of the process.
It's up to us to accept this lack of revelation whose empty
certainty must uphold our neutrality. Let there be objective
questioning where our confusion will not retreat. This very
lack of explanation should not be taken as a synonym for a
better hidden secret (which can eventually be brought to
light), but rather as an indecision which is by its fundamental nature insurmountable. It is insurmountable because
the "other" texts appear outside of the revelation only to
the extent that "certain" ones have been explained. However, this explanation leaves "unexplained" the limpidity
of *La Vue* or the need for a meticulous explanation to fortify,
it seems, the long didactic discourse of *Nouvelles Impressions*.
It's the gesture of unveiling which casts an inevitable
shadow, and henceforth deprives so many calm texts of the
possibility of having an indelible secret. The certainty of a
secret must not be placed on the same level as a probable
secret, but carried to extreme, the questioning brings out
the evidence of the relationship of revelation to its shadow.
It is to this relationship (and not to the hypothetical symmetry of secrets) that we must address our questions.

The texts outside of the process are up against the revelation of the process of which they form the opposite side,
the necessarily dark half. Whatever in them is invisible became so (and visibly such) when it was shown what was
invisible in *Impressions* and *Locus Solus* and in the plays. This
invisibility which is rooted in the revelation is nothing more
than the pure and simple visibility heightened by the indif-
ferent gesture of revelation. In these texts that were not
explained, which retain their original enigma of a solution
that comes from elsewhere and is applicable elsewhere, the
visible and the invisible are intimately mixed. But that's to
say little: for in the inextricability there could be a subtler
interplay of the secret; in fact, the visible and the invisible
are of the same material and of the same indivisible sub-

stance. Light and shadow are from the same sun. Invisibility is made evident by the visible. It owes its absolute transparency to the fact of not being exposed, which leaves it, when it comes into play, in the shadow. What hides that which is not hidden, what exposes what cannot be revealed —no doubt that is the visible.

The enigma inherent in the visible (which makes it essentially invisible) is that it cannot be discussed on its own terms, but from a distance which proscribes or permits invisibility. What is known about the process and about all the language which is placed under its heading will not serve as a key to decipher that which has no key, but will open to us by its very distance the space through which we can see what the original blinding visibility, equal in all its aspects, solar in each of its parts (similar to the *aqua micans* of Canterel's crystal), prevented us from seeing. The revelation of the process has cast its shadow on all the works outside of the process; but it has established that gray dimension at the limit of which is finally revealed to the observer what had already been shown where the brilliance was blinding.

La Doublure, La Vue, Le Concert, La Source, Les Têtes de Carton, and *L'Inconsolable* are spectacles, pure spectacles without respite. Objects are displayed in a profusion which approaches and yet is far from what constitutes the theater. Nothing exists which isn't visible and which doesn't owe its existence to the fact of being seen. But in the theater the visible merely forms the transition to language where it is entirely directed. In Roussel's spectacles the direction is reversed: the language turns toward things, and the meticulous detail it constantly brings forward is reabsorbed little by little in the silence of objects. It becomes prolix only to move in the direction of their silence. It is as if a theater was being emptied of everything that makes it comic or tragic, spilling out its useless decor, haphazardly pell-mell, before an unpitying sovereign and disinterested observer. It is a theater which had fallen into the inanity of spectacle and only offered the contours of what could be seen: the carnival, with its cardboard treasures, its colored papers, is the static, miniature, and round scene of a souvenir lens.

But this slight visibility dominates triumphantly. What doesn't it offer in its inexhaustible generosity? The vignette is in the letterhead of a sheet of the stationery often found in the lounges of hotels, placed in small, narrow black boxes which are open and divided into two compartments, the other destined to hold the envelopes. The poem *Le Concert* enabled me to count in the scene eighty-seven characters (I may be mistaken) perfectly recognizable by their appearance, their gestures, what they're doing, their concerns at times, often their professions, and their personalities as seen by their expressions. In addition, there is an indeterminate number of orchestra musicians (one can distinguish the violin bows, their uneven alignment, the sweeping motions which brought them to different heights), the audience, groups of strollers, customers around the coconut stand, children who are there "frolicking." This is not all: there are, besides, horses, a lake, boats on the lake; not far from there an omnibus, trunks, grooms. I forgot the hotel, "massive, high, immense," which eclipsed everything, "it was so colossal, monstrously vast." Around it "nothing is there for contrast." This small vignette on the letterhead is like the circular lens embedded in a souvenir pen, or the label on a bottle of Evian water, a prodigious labyrinth when seen from above. Instead of concealing, it naïvely places before one's eyes a network of paths and boxwood hedges, long stone walls, the masts, the water, those minuscule precise people going in all directions with the same fixed step. Language needs only turn to these silent figures to attempt through infinite accumulation to recreate that flawless visibility.

In truth, all these things need not be highlighted: it's like placing these things in a deep perspective. No great effort is needed to make them reveal their secret: an autonomous movement brings them forth, displaying what they are and even a little more. What is seen overlaps both the past and the future, creating a temporal vibration which doesn't negate but rather increases their hieratism. They do not only stand at this point in time, defined by a glance, but rather in ever-deepening layers wherein lies their whole being, with all its possibilities. A gesture, a profile, an expression reveal nothing less than the whole nature and this form wherein being and time confirm one another. Here, for example, on the pink label of a bottle of mineral water:

> A big woman
> With a prudent, cool demeanor, has, happily for her, a high
>   opinion
> Of herself and is never intimidated.
> She believes she knows almost everything; she is a
>   blue-stocking
> And pays no attention to people who read little.
> She is decisive when literature is discussed.
> Her letters, without an awkward word, without any
>   corrections,
> Are finished only after many laborious drafts.

Nothing of what is seen here is given nor can be given visually. This visibility is self-contained and offers itself to no one, drawing an interior celebration of being which illuminates it from head to toe for a spectacle without possible spectator. It's a visibility separate from being seen. Although access to it is through a glass lens or a vignette on a label or a letterhead, it's not to stress the interception of an apparatus between the eye and what it sees, nor to insist on the scene's lack of reality, but as the result of reduction, to place the act of seeing in parentheses and at another level. Due to this interception, the eye is not situated on the same plane as the things seen; it cannot impose on them its point of view, nor its habits, nor its limits. It must, without any intervention, let them "be seen" by virtue of their being; there's invisibility only within its own space. The conclusion of *La Source* underlines this effect so that it can't be ignored; the last figure on the label shows a man reading a letter; everything about his character is made known—his egotism, his fear of infection, his distrust of doctors, his taste for medicine, the smugness of his self-pity. Suddenly a hand, "horrifying and agile," reaches out and takes away the bottle of mineral water (to which the label is pasted); vision is restored to its natural dimension—the rule of distance bordered by the imperceptible:

> The American, sprawling more than ever, lights
> A cigar; the excited couple, over there,
> Always whispers things one can't hear.

The space registered by looking at "the real" is shadowy, hazy, in layers, and deep, and circled by darkness in the distance. Within the magical circle, on the contrary, things appear in their insistent, autonomous existence, as if they were endowed with an ontological obstinacy which breaks with the most elementary rules of spatial relation. Their presence, like a boulder, is self-sufficient, free of any relation.

There is a fundamental lack of proportion: seen the same way are the porthole of the yacht and the bracelet of a woman chatting on deck, the wings of a kite and the two points formed by the tips of a stroller's beard raised slightly by the wind (which is very strong at this spot on the beach). (Happily the *Nouvelles Impressions* will teach us not to confuse objects of such different sizes.) It's understandable why the cardboard heads were so attractive to Roussel: they systematically destroyed proportion by superimposing an enormous face on a body which then looked small as an insect, and the vivid colors of the beings emphasized an imperceptible detail which barely existed. The same effect is used in selecting names for the characters (Father Vulcan, Mrs. Embroidery, Young Drawer): the assimilation of things and people, the minuscule and the immense, the living and the inert, within one neutral being who would be at the same time disproportionate and homogenous.

La Vue, as if in immediate contradiction of its title, opens up a universe without perspective. It combines a vertical point of view (which allows everything to be embraced as if within a circle) and a horizontal point of view (which places the eye at ground level where it can only see what is in the foreground) to such an extent that everything is seen in perspective, but each thing, however, is seen frontally. It is a perspective simultaneously from the front and from above which allows, as in the works of certain primitive painters, an orthogonal presentation of things. There is no privileged point around which the landscape will be organized and with distance vanish little by little; rather there's a whole series of small spatial cells of similar dimensions placed right next to each other without consideration of reciprocal proportion (such as the cells for resurrection in *Locus Solus*). Their position is never defined in relation to the whole but according to a system of directions of proximity passing from one to the other as if following the links in a chain: "to the left," "in front of them to the left," "above, higher," "further," "further continuing on the left," "at the end of the beach," "still close enough to them," "a little more on the left on the other side of the arcade." Thus spreads the sand of *La Vue*, in discontinuous grains, uniformly magnified, evenly illuminated, placed one next to the other in the same noonday sun—already *La*

Poussière de Soleils. Near or far, the scenes are of the same scale, seen with the same precision, as if each had an equal and inalienable right to be seen. It happens, of course, that one figure placed in front of another will hide it (the foam on the waves blurs the outline of the rocks; a high wave hides three quarters of a boat): but these are surface effects, not effects of depth. The disappearance of form is not due to the essential rules of perspective, but to a sort of competition where other forms impose themselves, still leaving the first ones a right to visibility which always culminates by passing through into the language with a strange power to circle around the obstacle that meant to hide it. In *La Source* a woman who is barely visible—she's half-hidden in a sedan chair—is described in twenty-four verses which inform us: she has an Oriental hairdo, she dressed hastily, she is harebrained but with a quick hand, she allows people to pursue her, she is not reasonable. To be seen is not a result of visibility, it's an aspect of nature which is endlessly affirmed. Once inside this nonspatial place, whether in the lens of the pen or on the label—in this fictional world, analogous to reproduction, created of vague markings printed on paper—a plethora of beings serenely impose themselves; the luminosity of the whole never diminishes. It is a perpetual, soft emanation, existing outside of time.

Everything is luminous in Roussel's description. But nothing there speaks of daylight: there is neither time nor shadow. The sun doesn't move; being equitable to all things, it is poised above each. Light is not a medium in which lines and colors are bathed, nor the element in which vision can find them. It's divided into two domains which are not related: there is a sovereign white light whose ultimate sweep delivers the being of things; and then, in sharp surface bursts, in a fleeting plan, lightning falls on the surface of things, forming a sudden stroke, transitory, quickly darkened, etching an angle or a bulge, but leaving intact, obstinately in place, in their earlier presence, the things that it illuminates—without ever penetrating them. This second light is never from the depth of things; it spreads over each thing in rapid bursts: "Rare and slender illuminations run on the water"; on a vanity table in front of a mirror, the two slightly parted blades of the scissors "are covered with reflections and brightness"; on a boat at sea a man is leaning on a railing, his left hand holding the metal rail which runs along the deck; on the first knuckle of his third finger he wears a ring "which in its present position flashes lightning." In this fragmented space without proportion, small objects thus take on the appearance of flashing beacons. It's not a question of signaling their position in this instance, but simply their existence. It's as if the great neutral light that sweeps over them and spreads them out to the very root of their being suddenly contracted, focusing on a point on the surface to form for a split second a flaming crest. The basic deployment of the visible resurfaces as the contradictory brilliance that blinds. The division here between the luminous being and the dazzling lightning forms a plan familiar to Canterel's technique; by right it could reanimate the whole past and make it fundamentally visible. However, only a momentary brilliance surfaces, so special, so intensified, that it appears as an enigma before a blinded glance.

And from one illumination to another the inventory is drawn up; its momentum is ambiguous. It's hard to tell whether the eyes are moving or if the things come forward of their own accord. This spectacle has an equivocal motion (half inspection, half parade) where everything appears still, both eyes and landscape, but where without guidelines, or design, or motor, they never stop moving, each in relation to the other. This creates a strange configuration, both linear and circular. It is circular since everything is open to view without any possible vanishing point, or hiding place, or openings to the right or the left, like the circular glass lens set in the pen which frames the small paper circle on which is printed the curve of the beach and the convex line of the sea; just as on the pink rectangular label covering the bottle of mineral water whose edges almost meet at the back, barely leaving a slender transparent strip on the other side of the picture. Along these meridians things appear in their fullness, forming concentric circles on the surface of the language where they manifest themselves; flowers increasing in size as they approach the center. But this inexhaustible wealth of visible things has the property (which both correlates and contradicts) of parading in an endless line; what is wholly visible is never seen in its entirety. It always shows something else asking to be seen; there's no end to it. Perhaps the essential has never been shown, or, rather, there's no knowing whether it has been seen or if it's still to come in this never-ending proliferation. Thus on the letterhead of the stationery, amid the strollers, the carriages, the hotel, the boats, the porters running errands, the vendors, how is one to know before the ending that beneath the huge coolie-hat roof of the kiosk, the group of seated men depicted as making rapid movements with their instruments, immobile, silent, are drawing with negative music the central figure of the image? It's that things present themselves in a parade, at the same time pressing one against the other, forming a virtually infinite straight line, but meeting again at their extremities, in such a way that there is no way of knowing just by looking at these figures (as in looking at *The Hunt* by Uccello) if these figures are the same or different, if there are more or if those from the beginning have already returned, if they're just beginning, or if they have been repeated. Time is lost in space, or rather, it's always absolutely positioned in this deep and impossible figure on the right, which is a circle: there what has no ending is revealed as being identical to what begins again.

Such was the celebration of the dead in *Locus Solus* and that of time regained on the beach at Ejur. But there the return was discursive and easily analyzed; there was the past and there was its new beginning; there was the scene and there was the discourse which repeated it by explaining it; there were hidden words and machines that surreptitiously threw them out again. In *La Doublure* and *La Vue* what repeats is given at the same time as what is repeated; the past with the present, the secret with the silhouettes, the performance with the objects themselves. That's the prerogative of the pictures or vignettes described by *La Vue, Le Concert,* and *La Source:* they are reproductions but so anonymous, so universal, that they bear no relation to any original model. No doubt they represent nothing other than what they are (they are reproductions without having to resemble anything); the duplication is internalized. The language speaks spontaneously in all these things observed without there being any ulterior duplicate texts where the language is divided and its destruction creates, separately, one from the other, the mechanisms or the scenes. The discourse which describes them in detail finally is the one that explains them. It's a discourse without any volume, running along the surface of things, adjusting to them by an innate adaptation without apparent effort, as if the luminosity that opens the heart of beings was in addition the source of the words to name them:

> My glance penetrates
> The glass lens and the transparent
> Backdrop comes into focus. . . .
> It shows a sandy beach
> Just when it is lively and colorful.
> The weather is beautiful.

With this beginning, what is seen is easily described; but also everything begins to speak with inexhaustible volubility in the clear circle of visibility. It is as if the language carefully applied to the surface of things to describe them were thrown out again by a prolixity inherent in these things. The laconic vocabulary of description is blown up by all the discourse of what usually is never apparent. Little by little this unwonted and chatty visibility takes over the whole field of perception and opens it up for a language that then replaces it: everything begins to speak a language that is visible, and its invisible content is made visible. From the figures drawn with one stroke rises a chirping as limpid as their still profiles, their immobile fingers. This chattering is not about to stop in the glass lens where *La Vue* holds, enclosed like a shell, the sound of waves. This is how the silent gestures of the man speak:

> He is walking between two fairly pretty women,
> Each of whom has taken one of his arms
> In a friendly way. . . .
> To strongly emphasize what he is saying,
> He struggles and does everything he can; he uses
> The short, uncertain and limited
> Freedom that remains to his wrists and hands. . . .
> He wants people to believe his version
> And above all that it not be thought he's exaggerating,
> That he deals with the subject in a high-handed, frivolous
>   way,
> When indeed he stays as close as possible
> To the strictest truth; he is successful;
> He is listened to attentively; he provokes
> A mood of humor, and due to the scenes he evokes,
> Their shoulders shake, convulsed with laughter.

These are the two limits of perception (three figures arm in arm, shaking with laughter); a whole verbal world dilates and brings the imperceptible into full view, and the simple thing that seemed, because of the words, to leap to the eye, now seems dispersed, on the verge of being lost in this rising verbal swarm. This is the opposite technique from the process: from duplicated and dislocated language the process creates a whole expanse of strange flowers, metallic, dead, whose silent growth hides the monotonous beating of words. In *La Vue* and the related texts, it's the things which are open in the middle that from their plenitude give birth to a whole proliferation of language as if by sheer excess of life. The words conjure up a mundane world of things (the same things) from one shore to the other, often childish in thought, in feelings, and of familiar murmuring. Just like the hollowness that alienates a word from itself when repeated, the process springs from the mass of machinery never visible, but exposed without mystery to be seen.

And yet this world of absolute language is, in a certain way, profoundly silent. The impression given is that everything has been said, but in the depth of this language something remains silent. The faces, the movements, the gestures, even the thoughts, secret habits, the yearnings of the heart are presented like mute signs on a backdrop of night.

A horse is heard neighing
Over there, in the distance. Without warning,
To make her turn around completely, he slowly pushes her
With his right arm, gently holding her tight,
While taking her by the left hand. He holds her
Without saying a word, looking at her. He has just stopped,
But she still doesn't understand
What he wants; now he sweeps her along,
Making her turn around him,
By giving her his arm to lean on;
And almost without knowing how, she finds herself
Turned in the opposite direction. He looks at her broodingly
Without a word, keeping his usual bearing.
They start walking again, with the sea on their left.

There is nothing else in this final detour (it concludes the carnival in Nice) other than the first opening of words and objects, their mutual coming to light, and this pause, a body pivoting around, the reversal of all perspective—the same things but in the other direction; that is, a closing off of what had been open, and finally the disappearance of what had appeared. This is the whole enigma of the visible and why language has the same origin as what it describes. But isn't this precisely the function of the process: to speak and to show in a simultaneous motion, to build up as if it were a prodigious and mythical machine this confused source of language and objects? In *How I Wrote Certain of My Books* one sentence seems to carry more weight: "I was led to take a random phrase from which I drew images by distorting it a little as though it were a case of deriving them from the drawing of a rebus." That is to say that the language is already fragmented, so that its separate units are used to create image-words, images that are carriers of a language which they speak and hide at the same time, in such a way that a second discourse is created. This discourse forms a fabric where the verbal thread is already crossed with the chain of the visible. This prodigious and secret interweaving from which a whole language and vision emerge is what is being hidden by the process beneath the narrative of *Impressions* and *Locus Solus*. This is what is revealed by *How I Wrote Certain of My Books*. In *La Vue, Le Concert*, and *La Source*, this spoken visibility was already fixed by an anonymous artifice onto a piece of paper before anyone has either looked or spoken.

It is precisely the glass lens, mounted on the souvenir pen, that offers the roundness of an infinite landscape. It's the marvelous instrument for constructing words which with a basic generosity gives out something that can be seen: it is a slender piece of white ivory, long and cylindrical, topped with a palette and a faded inscription; and toward the bottom, an ink-stained metal band. A lens hardly larger than a brilliant dot opens, in the middle of this instrument manufactured to draw arbitrary signs on paper, not less distorted than itself, a space of luminous, patient, simple things. It is the pen of *La Vue,* and none other, that will write the works using the process, because it *is* the process, or to say it more precisely, its rebus: a machine to show the reproduction of things, inserted within an instrument for language.

The network of things and words which produce, like mushrooms of no known species, the figures of *Impressions* and *Locus Solus,* and which remains obstinately hidden in these texts, now is naïvely visible where it was made to be seen; it is even designated by a flagrant reproduction of the text which is called, so that no one can mistake it, *La Vue.* It is recognizable in this instrument for words, in this lens of the invisible, in this infinitely chatty landscape; it is another *métier à aubes* (work at dawn). But this one is even earlier; it's the process at dawn, with a naïve and savage brightness; the process without any procedure, but so evident that it remains invisible. The other, the one at noon, has to be well hidden in order to be seen. And perhaps its own reduplication will cast a shadow on what had never been veiled.

But one can go further back into the dawn of language and things: up to that first light seen to shine at the beginning of *La Doublure.* Even before offering things in their fullness, this brilliance surreptitiously reduplicates and opens them from within. This first flash is the one seen to shine when the actor at the beginning of the text tries in a solemn and inept manner to place the blade of his sword back into its sheath:

> With a sweeping, exaggerated gesture,
> Raising his gloved hand in the air,

He lowers the blade, which casts a flash,
Then tries to introduce it; but it trembles and fidgets,
His hands cannot make them meet,
The point and the opening of the black leather sheath
Which is turning, both seeming to flee one another.

This small clumsiness, this hitch in a simple gesture tears open the whole length of the fabric of things. Immediately there is a split in the spectacle, and the attention of the spectators is twice as concentrated and yet has shifted: their eyes do not move from the performance presented to them, but they recognize that imperceptible division which makes it a pure and simple spectacle. The assassin with the rapier is only an actor, his weapon a prop; the anger is feigned; his solemn gesture has been repeated a thousand times and shows that it is mere repetition by this slight shifting which makes it different from everything that has preceded it. But this spectacle, a duplication by its very nature, is yet even more profoundly a duplicate: the bad actor is only an understudy who wants to take the role of the great actor he is replacing. He only demonstrates his mediocrity as an understudy. It's within this space opened by the initial flaw in the duplication that the narrative will come into its full dimension.

After the episode of the clumsy gesture, we pass to the other side of the curtain, backstage, and then into the reverse of the life of an actor (the miserable room, the faithless mistress: she fell in love with Gaspard on seeing him in the role of a hoodlum, which he is unable to act out in reality; but she lets herself be kept by wealthier lovers, for whom Gaspard again is only a substitute). The main event takes place in Nice one afternoon during carnival, at the parade of masks—these cardboard duplications that Gaspard and Roberte watch without participating, both casting glances at them. But they themselves are reduplicated, since they are masked spectators. That evening after the parade they walk the streets strewn with confetti, refusing to take part in the festivities which are continuing around them, in order to remain alone. It's the reverse of the carnival; it's in the quiet night, the dark facet of this noisy day. Suddenly fireworks explode in the darkness, creating a sun in the middle of the night and reversing the order of things. In the last pages Gaspard has become an actor in a traveling troupe performing at the Neuilly Fair; it's the last caricature of carnivals and theaters in the poem. Between the crowd shoving in search of amusement, and the cardboard flats, he stands there on the wooden platform without curtains, which is nevertheless at that moment an empty stage—the visible reverse side of a play that has not yet been performed. It's a duplicate being reduplicated: no more than a silence, a glance, slow-motion gestures made in the empty space beneath the masks.

> Gaspard steps forward on the platform and sees
> A chair, its legs up,
> Lying on the left slightly above the stairs, useless
> As straw. He first picks it up by one leg,
> Then grabs the back and sets it down at the edge of the
>   platform, so to speak,
> With the back leaning against the railing.
> He straddles the seat as if on horseback,
> Feeling the back of the chair very flat and straight
> Cutting into his arms as he hugs it tightly;
> And then again he stares into the emptiness.

Seated on an empty stage—neither as a man nor as an actor, stripped of all his roles but also separated from himself—Gaspard is exactly the neutral moment which separates and unites the duplicate and the duplicated; his existence defines the black space that lies between the mask and the face it hides.

The whole description of the parade (which takes more than two hundred pages) resides in this minute space between the two. Apparently Roussel narrates only the most visible colors and shapes, and the illusions they create. But he never fails to point out the slightest flaw (imperfections, failures, unreal details, exaggerated caricatures, wear and tear, flaking plaster, awry wigs, melting glue, rolled-up sleeves on the dominoes) by which a mask denounces itself as only a mask, a double whose being is reduplicated and thus returned to what it is ordinarily.

The cardboard figures depict in a marvelous way what they mean to say. This huge blue cylinder with its shadows and reflections could easily be mistaken for the pharmacist's phial (here, as in the lens but in reverse, the lack of proportion is easily inscribed in the object's existence); this enormous man weaving along with a huge red face, how not to notice that he's the drunkard? But as he comes closer it is more discernible that "between the points of his collar, very far apart, and beneath a prominent Adam's apple," a small black aperture indicates the place of the real person and the window of perception. In the same way it's quickly noticeable that in the pharmacist's phial one can see:

A very dark rectangular opening
On the label in the middle; it's the hole
That's unsuspected at first from afar, through which
The man enclosed alone can see;
And from the bottom of the bottle to the ground, his lower
    legs showed
So that he could direct himself in the crowd.

It's in this necessary opening that the whole ambiguous nature of the mask is summed up: it enables the masked person to see (others and the world are no longer masked for him) and take in the impression made by his mask (in this way it becomes indirectly visible to his own eyes). But although it enables others to be seen by the mask, because of it, they see that it's a mask and nothing more. This tiny opening into which the whole mask can vanish is at the same time what displays it fully for viewing and the basis of its real being. It's the flaw which reduplicates the double and immediately restores it to its marvelous oneness.

But the play beneath the mask is brought to the surface, raised to the second degree, and proclaimed by language: the mimers carry signs which by a strange duplication announce what is visible to all. "I have a cold" is held above the head with a red nose that leaves the spectator without any doubt; in the arms of a white mother a black baby announces "the newborn accuser." It's as if the role of language were, by duplicating what is visible, to make it evident and thus to show that in order to be seen it needs to be repeated by language; words alone root the visible in the concrete. But what confers this power on it, since it is also painted cardboard of the carnival? Isn't it analogous to a mask multiplied by itself and endowed, like the flaw of vision, with a strange capacity: that of showing the mask and of duplicating it at the instant it reveals its simple being. In spite of being brandished above the masks, like the opening for looking out, language is that space by which a being and its duplicate are united and separated; it's a relation of that hidden shadow which shows things by hiding their being. It's always more or less a rebus.

The poem offers several examples of this verbal rebus where words are embodied in things within an inseparable but ambiguous network. For example, there's an enormous head opening its mouth wide to sing a *Marseillaise* that is never heard (one knows it because he carries a sign with musical notes: "only one sharp" and "several *res*"). He walks:

    With the bearing of a warrior,
    Having only a very thin fringe of hair,
    Being immensely bald without appearing old.

He holds out the tricolored flag on which he has written: "I am bald, humph!" (*Je suis chauve, hein!*).

Those without taste for word play will think what they will of this pun. Whoever has read Roussel can't help but find it remarkable: detail by detail, it has the outline of the miss with reiter in teeth *(demoiselle à reître en dents)* or of the whale with island *(baleine à îlot)*. It presents the same duplicate figure of speech within which resides a visible image produced by the distance between the two words. But it must be noted here that the two homonyms are present and understandable, and that the figure is amphibiological (baldness and chauvinism are clearly juxtaposed). It constitutes a rebus with a double meaning; it's a mask crossing appearance and being, the "seeing" and the "being seen," the language and the visible. It's necessary to recognize that this is a small preliminary model of the process, an entirely visible model, the process being this same image with half of it hidden.

Roussel's whole work up to *Nouvelles Impressions* revolves around a singular experience (I mean that it must be stated in the singular), the link between language and this nonexistent space which, beneath the surface of things, separates the internal from the visible face, and the external from the invisible core. There, between what is hidden within the evident and what is luminous in the inaccessible, the task of language is found. It's easy to understand why André Breton and others after him have seen in Roussel's work an obsession with the hidden, the invisible, and the withheld. But it's not that his language wants to conceal anything; it's that from the beginning to the end of its trajectory it resides constantly in the hidden duplicate of the visible, and the visible duplicate of the hidden. Far from making a fundamental division between what is divulged and the hidden meaning, like the occult language of the initiates, Roussel's language shows that the visible and the not visible repeat each other infinitely, and this duplication of the same gives language its significance. This is the function it has the moment it begins among concrete objects, and it is the reason that things are perceptible only through language.

But this sweet shadow which beneath the surface and the mask makes things visible and describable, isn't it from the moment of birth, the proximity of death, that death which reduplicates the world like peeling a fruit?

7
The Empty Lens

AT THE OPPOSITE END of Roussel's works, outside the domain of the process that neither *La Vue* nor *La Doublure* was acquainted with, forming beyond Ejur and *Locus Solus* a space as enigmatic as that of the early works and, like them, secret without having any secret, there is *Nouvelles Impressions d'Afrique.* Roussel devoted more time to it than he spent on the *Impressions* and *Locus Solus,* more than was required by *La Vue* and *La Doublure:* he worked on it from 1915 to 1928. However, in *How I Wrote Certain of My Books* Roussel invites the reader to make the following calculation: if, from the 13 years and 6 months that extend from the beginning to the completion of *Nouvelles Impressions d'Afrique,* you subtract the 18 months dedicated to the plays *L'Étoile au Front* and *La Poussière de Soleils,* and if from the remaining 12 years you subtract 5 times 365 days for another parenthesis (absorbed by a preliminary work now vanished from the oeuvre, having remained in manuscript), well, "I can state that it took me seven years to write the

version of *Nouvelles Impressions d'Afrique* as the public finally
saw it." The meaning of this arithmetic is not clear: Is it a
question of showing the extent of his labors? Or is it that
due to the timely subtractions we again find the cycle of
seven years which were those of *La Doublure* and *La Vue*
(1897–1904), then that of *Impressions* and *Locus Solus* (1907–
1914), the last work thus forming, when the nonpertinent
have been removed, the third period of seven years which
divides (naturally or by deliberate plan) Roussel's life. Or
perhaps he wanted to make known the system of parentheses in which this work—itself with parentheses—encloses
others and in turn is contained. It is symmetrical with the
early texts, framing the works dominated by the process in
a sort of parenthesis that exalts them and sets them apart.
In the same way, the two plays were bracketed, as both were
written during the intense period of writing *Nouvelles Impressions*, but according to a completely different technique.
As for the five years of work which inaugurated the composition and opened its parentheses, it has left residual and
elliptical signs silent beneath the text that it caused to be
written. The marvel is that this pattern of parentheses
which serves as signs to the *Nouvelles Impressions* gives the
irreducible remainder of the number seven. But this should
be accepted as Roussel presents it:

> *Nouvelles Impressions d'Afrique* was to have contained a de-
> scriptive section. It concerned a charm, a miniature pair of
> opera glasses whose two lenses [Stanhopes], each two milli-
> meters in diameter and meant to be held up to the eye,
> contained photographs on glass depicting the Cairo bazaars
> on one lens and the bank of the Nile at Luxor on the other.
>
> I wrote a verse description of these two photographs. It
> was, in short, a follow-up to my poem *La Vue*.
>
> This initial work complete, I returned to the beginning to
> polish up the verses. But after a certain time I realized that an

entire lifetime would be insufficient for such a polishing, and I abandoned my task. In all it had cost me five years' labor.

This passage is ambiguous. The pages of *How I Wrote Certain of My Books* that pertain to the works of the process are brief, but luminously succinct. While not telling everything, they leave nothing obscure: they are absolutely positive. These are negative—indicating the *Nouvelles Impressions* are not constructed according to the process, that they do not describe a view in a miniature binocular charm, abandoning five years of work, after considerable expenditure of labor. It seems as if Roussel could only speak about the shadow cast by the work, the part of it obscured by the brilliance of the actually written language, its black border. No doubt revealing the secret of writing which had created *Impressions* and *Locus Solus* shed some light on what remained in the shadow, but this shadow was an integral part of the language; it formed the dark core, and to bring it forth was to make the work speak in its original positivism. For the *Nouvelles Impressions*, clarification is, or appears to be, external, describing the work in terms of what is excluded in order to define it, opening a parenthesis that remains empty. It's as if on this last page of his revelation, by a worrisome and surprising move, Roussel has placed before our very eyes a pair of glasses whose lenses remain opaque.

It is true that the construction of the last work is as obvious as that of the first. It is easy to understand, only difficult to explain. Here is a group of five alexandrines:

Rasant le Nil, je vois fuir deux rives couvertes
De fleurs, d'ailes, d'éclairs, de riches plantes vertes
Dont une suffirait à vingt de nos salons
D'opaques frondaisons, de fruits et de rayons.

Skimming the Nile, I see two shores passing covered
With flowers, wings, flashes of lightning, luxurious green
     plants
One of which would suffice for twenty of our drawing rooms
Of opaque fronds, fruits, and sunbeams.

After these twenty drawing rooms (all decorated with the
foliage of one plant), let's open a parenthesis (reason
doesn't matter for the moment, and let's not say too quickly
that there will be an explanation, a clarification):

> . . . à vingt de nos salons
> (Doux salons où sitôt qu'ont tourné les talons
> Sur celui qui s'éloigne on fair courir maints bruits)
> D'opaque frondaisons, de rayons et de fruits.

> . . . in twenty of our drawing rooms
> (Sweet drawing rooms where as soon as one turns on one's
>   heels
> Different rumors are spread about the person leaving)
> Of opaque fronds, sunbeams, and fruits.

A happy transposition in the last syllable restores a positive
rhyme. On the trail of these heels, another parenthesis is
opened:

> (Doux salons où sitôt qu'ont tourné deux talons
> ((En se divertissant soit de sa couardise
> Soit de ses fins talents, quoi qu'il fasse ou qu'il dise))
> Sur celui qui s'éloigne on fait courir maints bruits)
> D'opaques frondaisons, de rayons et de fruits.

> (Sweet drawing rooms where as soon as one turns on one's
>   heels
> ((By making fun either of his cowardice
> Or of his subtle talents, no matter what he does or says))
> About the one who leaves, rumors are spread)
> Of opaque fronds, sunbeams, and fruits.

And there's a continuing elaboration within the text:

> (Doux salons où sitôt qu'ont tourné deux talons
> ((En se divertissant soit de sa couardise

((((Force particuliers quoi qu'on leur fasse ou dise
Jugeant le talion d'un emploi peu prudent
Rendent salut pour oeil et sourire pour dent))) . . .

(Sweet drawing rooms where as soon as one turns on one's
  heels
((By making fun of either his cowardice
(((Particularly strong whatever one does or says to them
Judging the punishment of an unwise action
Returning a greeting for an eye and a smile for a
  tooth))) . . .

At any rate, the poem concludes with the opaque fronds, the sunbeams, the fruits, which along with the wings, the flashes of lightning, the flowers and plants form the spectacle (beyond the forest of concentric parentheses), the visible border of the poem. The thickening can increase up to the fifth degree: five parentheses enclosing a language said to be of the fifth degree, the original sentence being degree zero.

But there are lateral forms of branching out: within parentheses of four degrees can be juxtaposed two budding developments of the fifth degree—two, three, or even more. Similarly, the third degree can carry several quadruple systems; the second, several triple systems, etc. The dashes must be included, a type of timid parenthesis, barely formed and still horizontal, with the alternating or simultaneous function of creating a feeble juncture or a break. Now they unite analogous terms enumerated, now they indicate a discrete incisiveness (acting as a half measure of containment), to evoke, for example:

. . . *Une eau—poison dont rien ne sauve*
Le microbe sournois chargé de rendre chauve—
Capable d'affamer les vendeurs de cheveux.

. . . A liquid—poison that nothing can save
From the cunning microbe responsible for creating baldness—
Able to bring out the greed of the hair vendors.

Finally, at the bottom of the page, as if at the roots of the text, there's a profuse branching out of notes, often very long: the fourth part of *Nouvelles Impressions* has only ninety-five verses of text, but one hundred thirty-four verses of notes. These are in alexandrines and arranged in such a way that as long as the reader reads them scrupulously in the indicated order, he will find a regular sequence of rhymes (the first verse of the note rhyming with the verse of the text to which it is appended, if it doesn't also rhyme with the preceding verse; and if the last verse of the note is suspended, it will rhyme with the first of the text in the order where it returns). It happens that a note will interrupt an alexandrine: the first words will complete the line, the transition to the note being nothing more than a stressed caesura. As for the note, it grows in a vegetal system similar to that of the text, slightly less vigorously, however, since it never surpasses the system of triple parentheses.

Thus the note on page 209 of *Nouvelles Impressions*, which begins proudly with the verse:

Nul n'est sans caresser un rêve ambitieux

There is no one who has not caressed some ambitious dream

originates in a passage of text already fortified by four parentheses and one dash (it's four and a half degrees); its own development forms a system of three envelopes and one dash (four and a half degrees since the note itself is one degree). Thus the heart of the verbal labyrinth is reached, guided by the straight line of verse and rhyme to the ninth degree of envelopment—the supreme degree never reached in any other summit of *Nouvelles Impressions*. In this eminent position of words, so protected in its restraint, so exalted by the pyramidal stratification of the levels of language, at once at the deepest and at the highest of this tower which is being dug like the shaft of a mine, a lesson can be formulated which is essential to understand after an itinerary which has crossed so many thresholds, so many openings and closings, so many broken discourses, right up to the issue of speech and silence:

De se taire parfois riche est l'occasion.

There are sometimes rich opportunities for remaining silent.

And if there is no tenth degree in this development of language which grows by backing toward the center, it is perhaps the opportunity seized and kept to remain silent— an opportunity as rich as a treasure and, like it, inaccessible.

I know that people won't fail to point out to me, and against me, the nine walls to surmount, the nine forms of test, the nine years of waiting, the nine stages of knowledge, the nine doors locked, then unlocked. What do they lead to if not to an initiatory secret, to the promised and reserved moment of illumination? By method and conviction I remain with the structure, noting only that according to the laws of harmony (that Roussel knew) a ninth chord cannot rise higher, and knowing that this form of the ninth can be found elsewhere in Roussel's work, giving his language not a theme but a number and a space from which he speaks.

For the moment let's admire another enigma. Roussel has calculated that on the average he worked for fifteen hours on each verse of *Nouvelles Impressions*. That's not difficult to understand when you take into account that every new ring of growth in the wood of the poem requires a reordering of the whole, the system only finding its balance once the center of this circular vegetation, where the most recent is also the most internal, has been finalized. With each additional increase this internal development couldn't fail to overwhelm the language it enriched. The invention of each verse was the destruction of the whole and stipulated its reconstruction.

Nothing is more difficult than to reduce this ever-circling turbulence, when compared to *La Vue*, where language had the task of faithfully following the contour of things, and by successive touches to refine the meticulousness of their details. As arduous as may be this patient and faithful reconstruction, what does it have in common with the permanent self-destruction of the language? Which is the most inexhaustible of these two forms of labor: to describe something or to construct a discourse in which each word that is created abolishes what went before? And yet Roussel chose the latter, finding himself incapable of finishing the first, whose completion—he believed after five years of work—would have indubitably required "a whole lifetime" and more. Strange that he should fail to accomplish again, twelve years later, what he had done without any apparent difficulty in *La Vue*, *Le Concert*, and *La Source*. It's all the more strange since the new work was less concerned with descriptions and the relationship of words to things, which is difficult in itself, than with "the polishing of the verses." The indefatigable measured alexandrines of *La Vue* had demonstrated, however, that Roussel easily launched "minimal barks of no importance," others animated "with motions seeming special and varied." He had no scruples about having men stroll along whose "extreme discouragement was complete" (the reason for leaning against "the parapet"); and finally from measure to measure in *La Vue* he had spread the most economical, the most indispensable language, equally the most "successful" on

> *Le souvenir vivace et latent d'un été*
> *Déjà loin de moi, déjà mort, vite emporté.*

> The latent vivid memory of a summer
> Already far from me, already dead, quickly vanished.

Why then this sudden opening of an impenetrable barrier between description and poetry, and perhaps between poetry and prose? Why sever the bond between two forms of language which are, as if in the wake of an internal collapse, separated by the emptiness of a time which a whole lifetime could not succeed in filling? And why did he choose between these two irreconcilable extremes the complication described above of parentheses and verses, to leave quietly, at the bottom of the text, without its ever appearing, the description which created it?

Another question: why is this text called, so notably, *Nouvelles Impressions d'Afrique,* presenting itself in this way as a repetition of a work with which it seems to have little rapport, and even less since it was not constructed, as the other was, according to the process? I don't think that the fleeting but all-encompassing descriptions of Damietta, of Bonaparte, of the gardens at Rosetta, nor even of the licked column in the temple of Aboul-Maateh justifies a title which relates more to Africa than to the incomparable skills of Ejur-on-the-Tez. What is the enigmatic bond linking the *Nouvelles Impressions,* the old ones (whose renewal the title proclaims but without any explanation), and *La Vue* (which was the basis of a first draft which remained secret, and whose existence was revealed only by Roussel himself)? The *Nouvelles Impressions* give the distinct impression of repeating the coronation of Talou and the sunny seashore embedded in the iridescent mother-of-pearl pen, but in a style that remained mysterious, which neither the text nor *How I Wrote Certain of My Books* explains directly. How to explain away the difficulty of this repetition whose discourse must cover such a great distance: the one separating the construction of machines for secretly repeating words (while triumphing over time) and the meticulous description of a world (invisibly visible) where space is abolished?

The four cantos of *Nouvelles Impressions* are framed along the periphery by thin rings that are visible. The doorway of the house in which Saint Louis was imprisoned opens the first canto which closes on "the old cathedrals," "the original cromlech," and "the dolmen beneath which the ground is always dry." A column licked by yellow tongues marks the threshold of the third canto. We already know between which shores, which wings, which palms in which drawing rooms, flows the last canto. The luminous crown of the second is like an image of the whole work: Bonaparte's little black hat is bursting like a darkened, eclipsed sun, with rays whose glory obscures Egypt, "her evenings, her firmament." In the same way the parenthesis that opens immediately with the first verses eclipses like a black disk the scene shown in the lens of the binoculars, leaving only a luminous corolla around the poem—which holds the eye by showing the flight of birds, the silhouette of a column against the sky, and the sky at twilight. *La Vue* was constructed along the exact opposite model: at the center the even lighting revealed things without any hesitation or shadow; all around—before and after this luminous display—was a circle of haze: the eye looked through the lens and placed in the shadows anything that was not part of the spectacle. At first everything was gray, but like a signal carrying its own source of light, the glance pierced the glass lens, and the backdrop came sharply into focus; the circle of white sand beach was as brilliant as the sun. Perhaps at the end the patient hand had trembled: "The brightness dims within the glass and everything darkens." In the *Nouvelles Impressions,* the sun is on the outside and circles the edge of the central darkness. In *La Vue* the shadows part like a curtain to let the light originate from its center.

In *La Vue* the absence of perspective increased the effect of a homogeneous light, creating small areas of equal brightness, whereas the eclipse of *Nouvelles Impressions* is made darker by the opposite effect of a perspective that's extremely sharp and deep: the opening of successive parentheses around a vanishing point which seems inaccessible. Starting from the foreground, each break suddenly forces the glance to pass to a more distant level, sometimes deep within the space, until the sentence forming the horizon line is finally brought back by the identical number of degrees to the right side of the picture, where for an instant can be found again the clarity of the beginning, which had quickly illuminated the thin portico from the left. This flight of the text toward a distant center is accentuated at every step by the construction of the sentences. They were smooth and horizontal in *La Vue;* they flowed according to a plan that exactly paralleled the spectacle and the movement of the eye that scanned it; their pace without ellipsis or abbreviation only had the task of uniting with the greatest verbal economy the least visible of the visible images. It was a matter of stitching things down with words of the greatest precision in a gesture where readiness is joined to caution, haste to an apparent ease, the straight thread with the sinuous line—rather similar to the motion of the seamstress described by sentences which follow the same curve as she makes:

> . . . A thimble
> Shines on her finger; with the edge of her thumb
> She pushes it with gentle pressure and raises it slightly,
> Only to let in fresh air, invigorating, pure.
> The needle she holds at the same time draws
> Across her work its fine, appreciable shadow
> Flowing over the sides; the very short thread
> Can't last longer, it risks
> A sudden ending; for it to be pulled out
> Of the needle, the least tug would be too much;
> The work is of good, delicate material,
> The thread comes from a soft hem nearing the end;

The material wrinkles, it's pliable and supple,
Frequently handled. . . .

The sentences of *Nouvelles Impressions* are constructed
very differently, their syntax following the outline of the
process of envelopment, in which they are trapped and
often isolated—thus they are formed as minuscule models
of the whole text. For example, this is the question that has
to be asked when two common ivory billiard balls, striking
each other, animate a billiard cue (what Roussel called "the
triggering process"):

> . . . *Pourquoi fière la bille*
> *Point ne fraie avec lui qui de rouge s'habille.*

> . . . Why the proud ball
> Does not click against the one clad in red.

The enveloping question shows with what care the meaning and the things are covered in the simultaneously elliptical and metaphorical language in which they are proudly
outfitted, like the ball in red. Objects are not presented for
what they are and where they are located, but rather described in their most extreme superficiality by a distant
anecdotal detail that designates them offhandedly, leaving
them within a gray parenthesis that is reached through a
labyrinthian detour, but from whence they never emerge
again by themselves. The soap offers its slippery body (it
must be remembered that Fogar demonstrated with such
skill its original properties, its simple forms, and its being
that is elusive and docile at the same time) only in two
forms—one is metonymic: "what helped clean him made
the bath flow," the other metaphorical: "what was heated
according to an order that was heard." Talou's black subject seen gamboling, all feathers deployed, around the incomparable prisoners, now suddenly becomes a "feathered
rooster of the human proprietors of the ark." Paradise be-

comes "a high, well-lodged flowery sojourn, making melodious choristers," unless it's preferable to encounter a
"smelly top tier of boxes at the theater." Thus the designation of things is scattered to their periphery, simply letting
loose a luminous and enigmatic ring circling around a black
disk which hides the simple being with the direct word.
Language has become circular and all-encompassing; it
hastily crosses distant perimeters, but it is always drawn by
a dark center, never identified, always elusive—a perspective extended to infinity in the hollow of words, just as the
perspective of the whole poem opens to the horizon at the
very center of the text.

Since *La Vue* the configuration of language has changed.
It was a linear language which spread slowly beyond itself,
carrying, in a regular flow, things to be seen. Now language
is arranged in a circle within itself, hiding what it has to
show, flowing at a dizzying speed toward an invisible void
where things are beyond reach and where it disappears in
its mad pursuit of them. It measures the infinite distance
between the eye and what is seen. The gracefulness of the
language in *La Vue* was that it gave the minuscule, the hazy,
the lost, the poorly placed, the almost imperceptible (and
even the most secret thought) with the same clarity as the
visible. The burden of the irregular, circular, elliptical language of *Nouvelles Impressions* is the inability to rejoin even
those things that are the most evident. Despite the unbelievable speed it has acquired in the characterization of
things, the beauty of it is that the ever-increasing accelera-
tion of this ontological flow sometimes throws out along its
path strange sparks as vivid as "the ignorant arrow with a
sublunar path," as bristling and erect as "the rooster who,
fleeing autumn, stamped with rage at the late dawn," as
gracious and thoughtful as that offered to a young woman
worker who "bites her finger, holding a rose," and shining
with a light so fantastic that by its brightness one could

mistake "a group of proud, caparisoned, rearing horses for a horde of aimless sea horses." All these rapid gleams fall in broken fragments, dark, enigmatic at the end of each canto, crowded one against the other like the voices of a fugue at the moment of stress:

> De mère sur la plaque elle se change en soeur))
> L'avis roulant sur l'art de mouvoir l'ascenseur)
> —Racines, troncs, rameaux, branches collatérales—
> L'etat de ses aïeux, les frustes cathédrales . . .

> She changes herself from mother to sister on the plaque))
> The notice pertaining to the art of running the elevator)
> —Roots, trunks, boughs, collateral branches—
> The state of his forefathers, the old cathedrals . . .

In terms of this race within its own space (which it hollows out and toward which it is vertiginously drawn), the language returns to the solid surface of things that it can cross once again, as in La Vue, following the current enumerations: the menhirs, the original cromlech, Egypt, its sun, its evenings, its firmament, the opaque fronds, its sunbeams, and its fruits. But this grace recaptured can only last an instant: it is the threshold—opened and closed as you will—starting from which is silenced a language which had spoken in the vain attempt to eliminate its distance from things.

In La Vue, Le Concert, and La Source the poetic foundation is a domain where a being is complete, visible, and calm. The scene presented may be the most illusory imaginable (the minuscule picture invisibly framed, the pure conventionality of an advertising vignette without any equivalent in reality). What it opens up is the dominion of a being completely frozen at the heart of its apparent animation; the movements are set apart from time, freed from it, and fixed beneath its flux. The crest of the wave swells without ever crashing in the tension of its breaking into foam; a stick takes flight from a throwing gesture and will never fall; and the ball, "fully inflated, bouncing and bright," laughs like a leather sun above extended arms which have already thrown it up and never will catch it again. The appearance of motion is caught in stone, but this immobility, this stone suddenly raised, forms a threshold through which language has access to the secret of being. Hence the privileged position Roussel always conferred on the verb *être* (to be)— the most neutral of verbs, but the closest to the common root of language and things (their bond perhaps, their common ground): "Everything *is* deserted and empty . . . ; after, it *is* a mound of large boulders . . . ; they *are* full of strange things, grouped in startling disorder; this entire strange section of the shore *is* primitive, virginal, unknown, and wild." And thanks to the marvelous power of the verb *être* the language of *La Vue* is maintained at the level of a descriptive epidermis striated with properties and epithets, but as close as possible to the being which becomes perceptible through it.

By contrast, the *Nouvelles Impressions* are characterized by a surprising rarefaction of the verbs; there are listings of nearly twenty pages where (aside from the relatives with their function as epithets) no verbs in a personal mode are to be found. There seems to be a succession of things in a void where they are suspended between a forgotten support and a shore not yet sighted. At every moment words are created from an absence of being, coming forth one against the other, alone, higgledy-piggledy, or by antithetical couples, or by pairs with analogous forms, or grouped according to incongruous similarities, illusory resemblances, series of the same species, etc. Instead of the state of being which in *La Vue* gave each thing its ontological weight, now only systems of analogies and opposites, resemblances and dissimilarities are to be found, where the being is made volatile, becomes sketchy, and ends by disappearing. The play of identity and of differences—which is also that of repetition (a repetition which is repeated in turn during the interminable lists Roussel places within his poems)—has eclipsed the lucid procession of beings throughout *La Vue*. The black disk invariably masks whatever there was to see in the four cantos of *Nouvelles Impressions*, and allows at the edge of each one only a thin, luminous ribbon. No doubt it is like a dark machine for creating repetition and thus the hollowing out of a void where being is swallowed up, where words hurl themselves in pursuit of objects, and where language endlessly crashes down into this central void.

Perhaps that is the reason why it was no longer possible to rewrite *La Vue*, to line up in horizontal and parallel verses a description of things that had lost the unchanging domicile of being and were excluded: the language escaped from within. It was to this flight and against this flight that Roussel had to address himself, casting verses into the void and not toward objects (now also lost with being) but in the pursuit of language, to construct a dam against this opening—at once a barred threshold and a new opening. Hence this gigantic effort, the last one made by Roussel, to make alexandrine verse out of a language that a central cavity twisted from within and sent toward this void. If Roussel had spent twelve years of his life to write fifty-nine pages (half as much as *La Vue* and the same as *Le Concert*), it's not that he needed all that time, indefatigable versifier that he was, to rearrange his rhymes with each new parenthesis, but rather, it was necessary at every moment to uphold his poetical language, inclined to turn inward toward the void, recalling the failure of a *Nouvelle Vue* (as admitted by Roussel), whose existence is now brought to mind. If by placing his eye to the lens of the binocular charm Roussel could not see things arranged of their own accord into alexandrine verses, if the lens was opaque, then there was an ontological failure which the repetitions of the *Nouvelles Impressions* mask and yet exalt at the same time.

But this is exactly where the *Nouvelles Impressions* repeat the old *Impressions.*

Talou's prisoners sought their freedom by constructing a world that was duplicated by its faithful imitation and made fantastic by the means used to accomplish the exactness of the copy. Each large *tableau* on the stage of the Incomparables was a sumptuous way of "returning to the same thing," and thus escaping the rule, playful, arbitrary, and cruel, in which the king of Ejur held his victims enslaved. There can be found imprisoned in the peripheral sentences of the *Nouvelles Impressions* motionless passages, or rather passages whose only movement is to pass from the same to the same. And just as Talou's white victims were granted their liberty and life by their marvelous duplication of the identical, the long chant of the *same,* then in the *Nouvelles Impressions* this is resolved as a return to the uniqueness of things which are seen and alive. The enumerations function as the machines and as the stage settings did in the other texts, but according to another plan: this vertiginous enumeration accumulates without stop in order to achieve a result which was already a given at the beginning but which seems to recede with each repetition.

The parentheses of the text contain vast thresholds through which parade the lines of analogous individuals or objects which have one aspect in common among themselves, which each in turn would show: 45 examples of things (or people) which become smaller; 54 of questions which it is difficult to answer; 7 signs which are not misleading when information is needed about a person, his character, his race, his medical record, or his social standing. These areas of analogy (what Jean Ferry quite correctly called the series) form a major part of the text: hardly one

twentieth of the second canto escapes it, a few light steps
are drawn leading to it. At first glance, the choice of these
areas, where, pell-mell, disembark a whole carnival of
incongruities, is in itself disconcerting. Why is it that on the
subject of Saint Louis' house at Damietta, in addition to 54
questions without answer, are enumerated 22 objects that
are useless to list as an overcoat for a native of Nice, and 13
props with which vain people want to adorn themselves
when having their photographs taken (like the pseudo-
traveler and an Eskimo parka)? In fact, despite the interruption of the parenthesis and the constant elusiveness of
the principal proposition—through them, and no doubt
due to them—the *Nouvelles Impressions* are structured with
the pomposity, the obvious coherence, of a didactic treatise, a treatise on identity.

I. The first canto begins at the threshold of a door, by
evoking things from the past which become present again
scarcely separated from their former selves by the divider
of a yesterday. Their identity is at the same time divided
and rejoined by time: witness the great names of history.
The canto of the identity approximates itself, but only af-
firms its imminent simplicity when its being is already lost
in the distance.

a. First category (54 items): Even with the most immediate things, can one be sure whether they are this or that,
useful or harmful, real or fake? Can he know "remaining
alone, Horace, at what speed to flee"? Would the young
writer know "until when his work would be published at his
own expense" (in fact, Roussel never knew)? It is confused
identity, the equation of contradictions, the secret of the
future and of the present itself (Does the drunkard know
"whether or not the bottles of Cliquot are waltzing"?).

b. Second category (22 items in footnotes): There are inversely things of different nature that come to rejoin one another to form a quasi-identity in which they repeat and nullify one another even though they appear contradictory. Does one pay when "for his payment he gets the hair curlers ready in the dark"? "When a lecturer introduces, to whoever is listening, a narcotic"? It's the reciprocal negation of things which in spite of their difference repeat each other.

c. Third category (13 items): When he is being photographed, the man tries to consolidate his identity by using unmistakable symbols in the hope that it will not escape him: the millionaire poses in front of the camera with her cabochon diamonds, the dry jockey (since he has not raced) "under his ample jacket of thin material with big dots." Each one in turn only reveals his mocking identity: an evident hollowness, a lie.

On the subject of names preserved by history, and of poses that have remained famous for posterity, let's consider Bonaparte with his hat, before the forty centuries of the pyramids. And thus:

II. The second canto. Its subject is change: modulation and permanence of forms, mutability in time, the shock of contradiction; but despite so much diversity, things obscurely remain the same.

a. First category (5 items): How many different objects can reproduce the form of a cross with extremely diverse significance?

b. Second category (40 items): How many things change proportion and are reduced in scale while remaining the same (from "the asparagus that's cast off after one bite" up to "having been on point, this gaudy ballerina")?

c. Third category (206 items): Among things of different sizes (a needle and a lightning rod; a fried egg and the pate of a tonsured monk ill with jaundice), there are similarities of form that could deceive a bewitched eye. Jean Ferry has explained admirably this enormous series, often extremely enigmatic.

d. Fourth category (28 items): Such contradictions in the life of the same person or the fate of the same objects (the glory Columbus conferred on the "anonymous" egg).

e. Fifth category (28 items): The sole idea of certain things is by nature contradictory (for example, the idea that "No one knew how to equal Onan by passing before all else the law of the giver giving").

f. Sixth category (2 items): A certain success is spoiled at the core by coming from a source that contradicts it.

Such contradictions can easily be found in the conduct and beliefs of mankind, which leads us naturally to the base of the superstitious column of

III. The third canto, "the column which, licked until the tongue bleeds, cures jaundice." This canto, as its title has already indicated, is consecrated to the relationship of things:

a. First category (9 items): Things that compensate for each other (the tightrope and the balancing pole).

b. Second category (8 items): Things that favor one another (the hand in the emperor's vest and the idea in his head).

c. Third category (6 items): The things that are made for each other, like the shepherd for the flock, the wax for the mustache.

d. Fourth category (9 items in footnotes): One thing indicates another, the way the frequenter of bars is betrayed "by the neatness of his strong horizontal jet [of urine]."

e. Fifth category (6 items): The real united with the false (an author can publish impressions of Africa "without having gone further than Asnières," which was not the case for Roussel, as we know).

f. Sixth category (6 items in footnotes): There are things which are unique and do not present analogies (for example, "the gold certain rams had in their fleece").

g. Seventh category (4 items): It is also restrictive compared to the first five; as in the case of belladonna, which is not useful when one has a glass eye, there are things which it is useless to bring together.

Thus things are sometimes unique, sometimes double, sometimes linked together, and sometimes solitary, discovering their identity and their essence often within and at times outside of themselves. They are separated from themselves and similar to themselves as are the two shores of the Nile.

IV. In Canto IV a slow barge divides the symmetrical unity of the gardens at Rosetta like a fruit cut open. There things are seen to be unique and yet similar to one another, ever different, but so close are the two shores of the river that when seen from above in the mirroring surface of the water, they appear like one another's reflection. But what is this barge which links these immobile and silent forms to its own motion and silently divides the two identical shores? What is it if not language? The first three cantos sing of the conflict and alliance of things; the fourth, the snare and diversion of words, the strange stars that outline and create fictitious but unsurpassable unities. How can the identical be found if it is quartered by language which toys with it and proposes another identity—the only one perhaps to which we have access? It's the song of the constellation of language. (This is my hypothesis: I cannot rid myself of the idea, entirely wrong perhaps, that the gardens at Rosetta are the site where formerly was discovered the Rosetta stone with hieroglyphics, which carried one message repeated in three languages. The river on which Roussel's barge moves forward is the antithesis of this solid block: on that stone three words meant the same thing; in the flow of language Roussel makes words sparkle, each of which by itself has many meanings.)

a. First category (6 items), *se faire à* (to adapt to): Shorn, the sheep becomes accustomed to the cold; on its perch the parrot adjusts to its chain.

b. Second category (15 items), *s'éteindre* (to extinguish): Ardors, fevers, desires, flames (even the one on the coward's backside).

c. Third category (3 items in footnotes), *progresser* (to advance or progress): The progress made by cannons over "awkward catapults"; horses, locomotives (the quarreling of sparrows).

d. Fourth category (8 items in footnotes), *se faire attendre* (to make people wait): The bridegroom when one is a girl without a dowry; the hollow plop of a pebble dropped into a well.

e. Fifth category (8 items in footnotes), *avoir un but* (to have a goal): A confused series, nonlinear, interrupted. What is certain is that "the slut set her sights on a coach" and a young priest, on purple robes (in truth the oyster in its travail is not aiming at the dickey of the elegant man).

It's in the paragraph dedicated to "goals" that Roussel's language attains its highest degree of envelopment, and within the ninth parentheses he takes the opportunity to speak of silence, as if that were the goal of the whole discourse, the minute black period aimed at in the midst of all these multicolored concentric circles; as if so many hard shells had been needed to protect and finally to display with this tender core of silence the "rich opportunity for remaining silent."

f. Sixth category (20 items in footnotes): A list of words with double meanings, such as *pâté*, "tears of an assortment of feathers" or a "tra-la-la timbal for robust gasters"; *champignon*, "suspicious food" or "chic support."

It is futile to insist on the extraordinary importance of this enumeration. Without any detours it leads to the first pages of *How I Wrote Certain of My Books* and to Roussel's revelation of the process. That is to say, it secretly leads to the first version of *Impressions*, for which it gives the key without ever stating it. It must be noted that none of the examples given in this passage is mentioned in the posthumous text (except *"blanc* [white]" used several times by Roussel in both meanings, explicitly announced: "the chalking of a billiard cue" and "civilized"); but it's easy to recognize in which texts the words mentioned here have played out their double meaning: *clou* (nail) and *bâton* (stick) in two of his early works; *se repentir* (to repent) in *Nanon;* *éclair* (lightning) perhaps served to strike Djizmé; *revolution* spun around a whole litter of kittens caught in the tentacles of a hysterical octopus (revolving kittens); *la suite* (of pages) organized Talou's parade; the *savon* (soap) served Fogar's skillful tricks; the *écho* caused Stéphane Alcott's bone-thin family to sing in unison, like the "echoes" one reads about in the "scandal sheets."

There's no doubt about it: the process had already been revealed when Roussel made his posthumous revelation. It was a long meandering through numerous identities and differences leading to this form which for Roussel was supreme, where the identity of things was definitely lost in the ambiguity of language; but this form, when dealing with the concerted repetition of words, has the power of creating a whole world of things never seen, impossible, *unique.* *Nouvelles Impressions* is the repeated birth of the old one— the theoretical and didactic summation of things and of words which necessarily leads to the creation of his earlier work. It is *Nouvelles Impressions* because, being younger than the first, it tells of its birth.

g. Finally, isn't the last category futile, after the two preceding ones? The subject is seven animals whose qualities have not turned egotistical: a ram that is not proud of becoming a goatskin. The reason is that the animals neither resemble words that have been quoted nor the vain people who were the subject of the first canto, which opened beneath the language an ocean of lost identity. Essentially, this ultimate category is not superfluous: at the moment the discourse leads us to the supreme surfeit and to the supreme source, there, at the bottom of the page, was to be found the thin, unexpected reassurance (or vertigo) of pure conscience lulled asleep, and guardian animals who without presumption maintain their paradisial identities, long after we have crossed and divided by our barge and our language the identical shores, the opaque fronds, the sunbeams, and the fruits.

This is the demonstrable coherence of this treatise: identity pursued, in things, forms, animals, and men, followed through resemblances across measure and immoderation, sought after at all levels of being, without concern for dignity, hierarchy or nature, displayed in composite figures, lost in others more simple, everywhere coming into being and fleeing in every direction. It's a cosmology of the *same*. It's a gigantic Noah's Ark (but even more welcoming), which takes in couples not to multiply the species but to pair off the most incongruous things in the world so that born from these figures in repose are unique monsters inseparable from identity. It's Genesis in reverse, which seeks to return to the dispersal of beings. Its interminable enumerations form horizontal dynasties, instantly dispossessed, where the most unexpected conjunctions attempt to reinstate the sovereignty of the *same*. As a result of objective irony it's only the repetition of these failed attempts which creates the hollow form of the identical, never assignable to a specific thing. It's as if language alone in its fundamental capacity for repeating and of being repeated could contribute what being had withdrawn, and could only give it while in full pursuit, going without pause from *one to the other*. What had been seen in *La Vue* (things as immobile as statues) is now only the meteoric passage, the invisible leap, the never-ceasing *lacunae of being* between this one and that one. Even when this language to which the last canto is dedicated states one thing, it could as well, with the same words, mean something else. This creates the final irony, that the very location and possibility of repetition, by re-

peating itself, does not remain identical to itself. Now
where can the treasure of identity be found if not in the
mute modesty of animals or in that which is beyond the
ninth level of language—in silence, unless it is used systematically to create a marvelous, unique language, the capacity to say two things with the same words. These are the
three possibilities opened by the language of the last canto
of *Nouvelles Impressions*.

Nouvelles Impressions is a type of dictionary devoted to the
rhyme of things: a treasury of what can be gathered together according to the rules of an ontological versification
in order to write the poetry of their being. The subject, as in
the early works, is an exploration of the empty and moving
space where words slide over things. But in the narratives
of repeated sentences, the ambiguity of words was methodically extended in order to bring out in a pure state, as the
birthplace of the imaginary, the "tropological" dimension.
This is now revealed as crawling with things and words
which call to each other, clash with, are superimposed on,
escape from, are confused with, or exorcised by one another. It's as if the glass lens, empty when it comes to
revealing the harmonious order of visible things and language, had now become fecund with all these gray shapes,
invisible, fleeing, where words ceaselessly play between the
meaning and the image. *Nouvelles Impressions* thus returns to
the classical treatise on grammar and rhetoric. It is an enormous anthology of the "tropological" figures of the language: "Every time there is a difference in the natural relationship which gives rise to a borrowed meaning, it can be
said that the expression which is based upon this relationship belongs to a specific trope." Such is the definition of
"trope" that Dumarsais formerly gave; it could as well be
the definition of all the figures that march by in Roussel's
interminable series.

This "treatise of lost identity" can be read as a treatise on all the marvelous torsions of the language: a reserve of antiphrases (Canto I, Series a), of pleonasm (I, b), of antonomasia (I, c), of allegory (II, a), of litotes (II, b), of hyperbole (II, c), of metonymy (all of Canto III), of catachresis and metaphor in Canto IV. As proof I will only consider the note in Canto IV which enumerates the words with double meaning so important for the genesis of the whole work:

> *Éclair dit: feu du ciel escorté de fracas*
> *Ou: reflet qu'un canif fait jaillir de sa lame.*

> Lightning is said to be: fire from heaven accompanied by noise
> Or: the flash made by the blade of a pocketknife.

Now this is what can be read in the chapter on homographs in *Homonymous Verses* by Fréville:*

> *—Dé qui sort du cornet m'enrichit ou me ruine*
> *Dé pour coudre sied bien au doigt mignon d'Aline*
> *—Jalousie est un vice, hélas, des plus honteux*
> *Jalousie au balcon déplaît aux curieux.*
> *—Oeillet petit trou rond sert pour mettre un lacet*
> *Oeillet avec la rose arrondit mon bouquet*
> *—Vers charmants de Virgile, ils peignent la nature.*
> *Vers rongeurs, tout hélas devient votre pâture.*

> —Dice which come from the shaker bring one wealth or ruin
> Thimble for sewing fits on Aline's pretty finger
> —Jealousy is, alas, one of the most shameful vices
> Shutters on the balcony offend the curious.
> —Eyelet is a small round hole for placing a lace
> Carnation with roses fills out my bouquet
> —Verses so charming by Virgil portray nature.
> Worms, devourers, everything alas becomes your pasture.

All these examples can be found in the works of Roussel; I even notice that the flying pile driver from *Locus Solus* was

---

* Fréville, *Les Vers Homonymes Suivis des Homographs* (Paris, 1804).

already present in Fréville, with the dual meaning of *demoiselle,* to which is added that of "dragonfly" (hence, perhaps, the gyrating wings on the paving instrument invented by Martial Canterel):

> *—Demoiselle se dit d'un insecte à quatre ailes;*
> *Demoiselle élégante a de riches dentelles;*
> *Demoiselle, instrument pour paver les ruelles.*

> —Dragonfly is called an insect with four wings;
> Young lady elegant with rich laces;
> Drill, a machine for paving streets.

It's irrelevant whether or not Roussel actually held Fréville's book in his hands, or another analogous to it. The essential thing is that across this undeniable relationship of form, *Nouvelles Impressions* appears as what it is: the inexhaustible crossing of the mutual realm of language and being, an inventory of the game by which things and words designate one another, miss one another, betray one another, and hide one another. In this way *Nouvelles Impressions* is related to all of Roussel's other works: it defines the space and location of language. But at the same time it profoundly opposes each of Roussel's other works: in the minute interstices of an identical language it creates narratives, descriptions, skills, machines, stage settings, strictly unique, destined to repeat things, or to repeat themselves, or even to repeat death. The marvelous detailed machines enveloped and made to appear natural the most startling meetings; it's the festivity of ceremonial weddings in which words and things contract among themselves and with each other, an alliance dedicated to infinite repetition. *Nouvelles Impressions* in search of impossible identities creates minuscule poems where words collide or separate, charged with opposing magnetic polarity; in one or two verses they cross an impenetrable distance between things, and from one to the other establish a lightning contact which throws them

back to their original position. Thus strange shapes spring
forward, sparkling for a moment, poems of a second's duration, where, in a spontaneous motion, the separation of
things and the emptiness between them is abolished and
reconstituted.

Poems of possible confusions:

> —*Quelque intrus caïman proche un parasol fixe*
> *Pour un lézard contre un cèpe.*
> —*Quand sur eux sans bourrasque,*
> *It s'est mis à neiger, des oeufs rouges massés*
> *Pour des fraises qu'on sucre.*
> —*Pour un cil*
> *Courbe évadé d'un oeil doux, une corne noire*
> *De chamois.*
> —*Un tuyau d'eau pour une épaule d'immortel*
> *Où rampe un cheveu long.*

> —Some intruding alligator near a fixed parasol
> For a lizard against a mushroom.
> —When on them without a squall,
> It began to snow on the piles of red eggs
> For strawberries being sprinkled with sugar.
> —For a curved lash
> Lost by a sweet eye, the black horn
> Of a mountain goat.
> —A water hose for an immortal shoulder
> Where lies a long strand of hair.

Poems of meetings without place:

> —*La boule aquatique et nue*
> *D'un dentaire effrayant recoin*
> —*Une oisive araignée explorant un chalut*
> —*L'odalisque à qui fut jeté le tire-jus.*
> —*Un cigare réduit à l'état de mégot,*
> *Le disque du soleil dans le ciel de Neptune*
> —*Prométhée aux fers dans le Caucase,*
> *Le chat dorloté puis cuit de la mère Michel.*

—Des doights nus d'écolier,
  Une poutre à décor funéraire.

—A bare aquatic ball
  Of a frightening dental cavity
—A lazy spider exploring a dragnet
—The odalisque to whom was thrown the juicer.
—A cigar reduced to a butt,
  The solar disk in the sky of Neptune
—Prometheus chained in the Caucasus,
  Mother Goose's cat, pampered then cooked.
—The bare fingers of a schoolboy,
  A pole with funereal decor.

Poems of strict grammatical economy which duplicate unbridled chance:

Quand naît l'orage à qui dominé le contemple
Et l'oit pour moins que la lumière ailé le son.

When the storm arises, whoever is caught contemplates it
And listens to it, less for the winged light than the sound.

In this clash of words and strange images, sometimes there's one that's suddenly perfect, such as this one of destiny:

Le mal qui foudroie en plein bonheur les toupies

The evil that strikes the spinning tops in their full happiness

or this other one of the throat:

Un cavernaire arceau par le couchant rougi
A stalactite unique.

A cavernous arch reddened by the sunset
Has a unique stalactite.

All this infinitesimal poetry delivers in a raw state the materials out of which formerly were meticulously constructed the machines of Ejur or of *Locus Solus*. Without the structure of long mechanical discourse, pebbles and flashes of light are dispersed here, erupting directly from the mine, the chaos of objects and words by which all language begins. The marvelous minerals which Roussel's works leave asleep within the depth of their discourse are now made visible, spread on the surface, a treasure restored to the inchoate language. The space discovered between the mask and the face, between appearance and reality, even in the ambiguous volume of words, this emptiness that had to be covered over with so many fantastic and meticulous figures, is revealed as replete with wealth fragmented into sequins: those that come forth, for a brief moment, against the night, from the dangerous twinkling of words and things. There in the imperceptible turns and minuscule shocks, the language finds its "tropological" space (that is to say of *turns* and *detours*), the poetry its resources, and the imagination its ether. The last picture with which Roussel illustrated *Nouvelles Impressions* depicts, against the darkness, a starry night.

Two additional words. Ejur's festivities were, as the text tells us, a "gala of Incomparables" (Incomparables, in fact, were the prisoners and their black friends, since they were unique in their talent for reconstructing exactly, and by any means, the unfailing identity of things). Well, what is *Nouvelles Impressions* if not equally a festival of Incomparables—the rapid dancing of a language leaping from one thing to another, bringing them face-to-face, and from their incompatibility setting off everywhere short circuits, firecrackers, and sparks. Incomparables, sparkling, innumerable, dispersed in the emptiness of language which brings them together and holds them apart—such as the figures strewn across the skies of *Nouvelles Impressions*.

The two plays, *L'Étoile au Front* and *La Poussière de Soleils*, which were written during the difficult composition of

Nouvelles Impressions, open a parenthesis, as it were, where one rediscovers the very structure of this last work, even though they are subject to the process. *L'Étoile au Front* is constructed as a series of analogies: a listing of modest objects whose illustrious origins place them in opposition to the tarnished glory which is evoked in the footnote to Canto III. Compared to this, which is brief, the play is at an infinitely developed level. *La Poussière de Soleils* is constructed like steps descending down a well to the treasure, parentheses within one another (three times nine if I'm not mistaken). Could it be said that the sequence of *La Poussière de Soleils* leads to a secret identical to the one revealed in the next to the last page of the poem, that is to say, to the process? Perhaps. In any case, what is surrounded by these triple parentheses squared would not be the marvels of a forbidden knowledge, but rather the visible form of its own language.

8
The Enclosed Sun

"HE'S A POOR little patient," said Dr. Pierre Janet.

This is a statement of limited insight coming from a renowned psychologist.

It would be inconsequential, in truth, if Roussel himself had not made a similar statement.

He broached the subject indirectly, recalling his illness and Janet's treatment with an indifference that only takes into account historical fact: he quotes *De l'Angoisse à l'Extase* as a remote anecdotal document. His first-person narrative in the posthumous revelation is already as cold as the third person which is implied by the nature of the subject of the book, and also perhaps in the stiffness of his language.

Apropos of the "I" which speaks in *How I Wrote Certain of My Books*, it is true that a disproportionate detachment at the heart of the sentences he pronounces makes him as remote as the third-person "he." They become confused in the distance, where self-effacement brings out this third person who has been speaking at all times and who always remains the same.

This is because death has already exercised its sovereignty. Having decided to do away with himself, Roussel defines the empty shell where his existence will be evident to others. Dr. Janet, the crises, the illness, are no more important than the success or failure, the controversial performances, the respect of the chess players, the social position of his family. These are the surface adjustments on the exterior of the machine, and not of the precise clockwork mechanism which secretly sets it in motion.

I believe on the contrary that Roussel exposes himself in this third person whose discourse is already solidified. He outlines in the direction of his death a passage that is symmetrical to the one Canterel invented to drill into the cadaver a return to life. He approaches step-by-step this *other*, this *same* that he will become on the other side of the impenetrable pane. And like the resurrectine, the cold of the language defines the images which are reborn indefinitely, articulating this passage from life to death through which the essential passes. He solemnly transmits the genesis of works whose kinship he defines with madness and suffering (so often seen in the anecdotes of *L'Étoile au Front*), which must be its stigmata of legitimacy.

How could Roussel make his work vulnerable to this devastating proximity when he was trying to gain "some posthumous recognition"? Why would he place in jeopardy a language protected for such a long time, and which would be preserved forever by the death to which he is exposed? Why, at the moment of showing it, this sudden bracketing of a delirium of truth? If there is a relationship between madness and death in this last work, no doubt it's to point out that at all cost, and as Roussel actually accomplished it in that gesture in Palermo, the work must be set free from the person who wrote it.

In the sparseness of his revelation, by contrast, he gives the central position to madness. Consider how the text develops: first there's the explanation of the process, then the autobiographical narrative. Between these two Roussel inserted three parentheses: the first brings up his illness; the second the greatness of Jules Verne; the third stresses the sovereign role of imagination in his works. And parentheses for Roussel have the quality of being open and closed at the same time, which is essentially related to the threshold. Within it what is stated is not merely adjacent, but definitive. With this triple threshold, what is it that is being set off if not the rigorous autonomy of language? It's the lack of relationship with the outside world ("from all my trips I have never gotten anything for my books"), empty space that words and their machines cross at a dizzying speed (Jules Verne "has raised himself to the highest peak attainable by human language"), the mask of madness beneath which can be seen this great luminous emptiness.

Roussel never spoke of his crisis as "madness in the eyes of the world." He never detaches himself from it. Rather, he shows that for a while at least he found his place: "For several months I experienced a feeling of glory of extraordinary intensity." He internally experienced being within a sun whose center he was. Roussel does not take into account other people's lack of understanding of his crisis. He speaks of it as a luminous hearth from which he is banished without reprieve. No doubt he perceived this sphere in the works of Jules Verne and it made all real suns disappointing. He suspended it above his posthumous revelation.

In fact, this solar experience during his twentieth year was not perceived from within as a form of madness. It's the opposite of the events that followed soon after, triggered by the lack of success of *La Doublure*. It came as "a terrible and violent shock," which was followed by "a frightful ner-

vous illness." It is only with this subject that the word
"illness" is used. I noticed another fact: on the subject of
Martial, Janet evokes a patient in his "forty-fifth year"
(that's the period of the writing of *Nouvelles Impressions*).
Roussel never says a word about this episode. He only cites
the pages of Janet's work that refer to Martial's states of
glory, not those which evoked more recent events (probably pathological even in Roussel's eyes). Only that first sun
in its ingenuousness belongs to the body of his work.

It's difficult to accept his divisions. These things form a
seamless material. During the period Roussel was working
on his first book, he experienced a feeling of universal
glory. It was not an exacerbated desire for fame but a physical state: "What I wrote was surrounded with luminous
rays. Each line was repeated thousands of times and I wrote
with thousands of flaming pen points." When the book
appears, all these duplicated suns suddenly are extinguished; the twining flames are absorbed in the black ink.
All around Roussel this language which was luminous in its
least little syllable, like a magical liquid, now was dissolved
in a world without attention: "When the young man with
intense emotion went out into the street and noticed that
people did not turn around as he passed, his feeling of
greatness and luminosity was suddenly extinguished." It's
the night of melancholia. However, this light will continue
to shine near him and from afar (as if from within a darkness that obscures distances and makes them unattainable),
dazzling or imperceptible according to an ambiguity characteristic of all his work. It will even give rise to this decision to die, to rejoin in one swift leap this marvelous point,
the heart of night, and hearth of light. All of Roussel's
language resides in this vain and obstinate place which
offers clarity from a distance. It gives glimpses of it, but is
strangely closed in on itself, asleep within its own porous
substance, which lets it burst forth at a long night's distance

that it never crosses: "This feeling of a moral sun, I was never able to regain it, I sought it and seek it always . . . I am Tannhäuser longing for Venusberg." Nothing in this sequence can be set aside.

That this sequence (or one of its curves) coincided with his illness is one thing. But that Roussel's language never stopped trying to abolish the distance that separated him from the original sun, that is another matter.

I don't want to return to a question that is tirelessly repeated. I am trying to find out if there is not, solidly buried, an experience where sun and language . . .

Such an experience presupposes that it's attainable, and whence can it be articulated except from this impure ground where his illness and his work are considered equivalent? He speaks in a varied vocabulary, crowded with qualities or changing themes which are sometimes evident as symptoms, sometimes as aspects of the style, or of the suffering or of the language, so that without great pains a certain definition can be formulated which is as valid for the work as for the neurosis. For example, the theme of opening and closing, of association and of dissociation, of the secret, of dreaded death conjured forth and preserved, of resemblance and imperceptible differences, of the return to being identical, of repeated words and many others which belong to the vocabulary of obsessions, leaves on the work the imprint of a pathological nervous system. It's easy to recognize the same outline in the rituals Roussel formed for every day of his life: he wore his collars for only one morning, his neckties three times, his suspenders for fifteen days; he often fasted so that food did not disturb his serenity; he wanted to hear talk neither about death nor about frightening things out of a fear that words carried the contagion of misfortune. His life, Janet said, is constructed like his books. But if so many similarities leap to the eye, it's because diverse forms have been isolated in order to be clearly perceived (rituals, themes, images, obsessions), which, belonging neither to the order of language nor completely to the order of behavior, can circulate back and forth from one to the other. It is then no longer difficult to show that the work and the illness are entangled and incomprehensible one without the other. The more subtle will claim that the work poses "the question of the illness," or rather, poses "the illness as a question." The game was played in the beginning: a whole doubtful system of analogies was given.

There is, however, the fact that the identity of certain forms presents itself as an obvious perception. Why refuse to see the same image in the cells for cadavers that Canterel had built in the middle of his solitary garden and the small glass opening that Roussel had set into the coffin of his mother, so that he could contemplate from the other side of time this cold life, offered up without the hope of an impossible resurrectine. The obsession within the work with masks, disguises, doubles, and duplications can be made analogous to Roussel's talent for impersonation, which he displayed early and to which he gave a slightly ironic importance. "I experienced the feeling of success only when I sang to my own accompaniment on the piano and above all when performing the numerous imitations I did of actors and of ordinary people. But at least my success was enormous and complete." It is as if the unique sun—which once formerly was of the body of his language—could only be rediscovered in the dividing of the self, in the impersonation of others, in this slight space between the face and the mask, whence sprang precisely the language of *La Doublure*, when the sun was still within him. Perhaps all the marvelous imitations presented by Talou's prisoners reflect Roussel's obstinacy: "He worked for seven years on each of his impersonations, practicing them when he was alone, repeating each sentence aloud to catch the intonation, imitating the gestures until he achieved a perfect resemblance." In this ascetic transformation into someone else, can't there also be found the incessant going back and forth of death within the cells of *Locus Solus?* Roussel deadened himself no doubt to be able to imitate this other life alive in others; and inversely by replacing the self with others, he imposed on them the rigidity of the corpse. The suicidal and murderous gesture of imitation recalls how much death is present in the work by the play of duplication and repetition of the language.

But are there other resemblances between these texts and his behavior, and is there something else, besides resemblance? Where do these images come from? And from what territory do they rise up? And on what ground are we standing in order to perceive them, certain of not being mistaken? What significance can a trail left in literary language or in a gesture have when by definition the work does not have the same meaning as everyday language?

In fact, none. There is no system common to existence and to language, for a very simple reason: language alone forms the system of existence. Along with the space that it defines, it constitutes the place of forms. Here is an example: as indicated, if Roussel showed death in the glass pane of a parenthesis, he willingly hid the secret of birth in the heart of a labyrinth. This is how he stated it for Dr. Janet: "Practicing forbidden acts in private rooms knowing that it is prohibited, risking punishment or at least the contempt of respectable people, that is perfection. But that nudity should be shown, and sexual pleasures can simply be seen at a public spectacle without risk of punishment, with the consent of parents, and while pretending to remain chaste and virtuous, that is unthinkable, inadmissible. Everything concerning love must remain forbidden and inaccessible." A relationship seems to appear between these statements and the secretly glorious births in *L'Étoile au Front.* I am aware that it cannot be taken literally. But in the context of the work, and fundamental to Roussel's experience of language, there seems to be a place where birth is hidden, the unique and illegitimate impediment, but it can also be a repetition that is always anticipating itself; it acts as a mirror in relation to death; before life, it gives a due date to be met but for a long time kept secret. The labyrinth of time is folded back upon itself, and within this darkened heart its invisible brilliance shines for no one. That is the reason why birth is beyond language and at the end of language. The words slowly return toward it, but can never reach it, since they are always a beginning and they are always a repetition. When they seem to have reached it, what do they bring to this empty place if not what can be repeated, that is to say, life repeated in death? Birth, which is excluded from the basic possibility of language, must also be removed from everyday meaning.

Thus it is not the theme of a sexuality carefully folded within a ritual which is at the origin of all these labyrinthian births so frequent in the work. Rather it is the relationship of a language that duplicates and is duplicated every morning in all its original purity. Birth is an inaccessible place because the repetition of language always seeks a way to return to it. This labyrinth of origin is not a visible result of his illness (a defense mechanism against sexuality) any more than it is the veiled expression of esoteric knowledge (hiding the way in which bodies can give birth to one another); it is a radical experience of language which proclaims that it is never quite contemporary with its solar origin.

What is meant by this experience, Roussel's pathological sensations or the core of his work? Or both at the same time, in one doubtful word?

Isn't the language situated between the work and madness, the place, empty and filled, invisible and inevitable, where they are mutually exclusive? In Roussel's early works language manifested itself as a sun. It placed things in sight and within reach, but in such a dazzling visibility that it obscured what it had to show, separated appearance and reality, the face and the mask with a thin sliver of light. Language, like the sun, is this brilliance which cuts, removes the cardboard surface, and proclaims what it says: it is this double, this pure and simple duplicate. The cruelty of this solar language is that instead of being the perfect sphere of an illuminated world, it divides things to introduce darkness into them. It is within this language that *La Doublure* takes its place. During this period the pathological feeling is that of an internal globe, marvelously luminous, which seeks to shed its light on the world; it must be safeguarded in its original space out of fear lest its rays lose themselves even to the depth of reaching China: Roussel shut himself up in a room with curtains carefully drawn. The language traces what is shared by these opposing images. The sun is enclosed, running the danger of being lost in the external night, and there the sun set free creates beneath each surface a little lake of night, shifting and disturbing. These two profiles facing each other create out of the same need the following figure: that of an enclosed sun. It is closed in so as not to dissipate itself, so that it will no longer divide things in two, but present them against the background of its own luminosity. It's the solar language held prisoner by the lens of *La Vue*, enveloping men, words, things, faces, dialogues, thoughts, gestures, all displayed without any reticence or secret within the circular glass lens. It is also the opening found within a unique and duplicated sentence, the calm microcosm of the circular stories. But this period of the domesticated sun, "placed in a box" that is opened at will and visible to the core by a piercing, sovereign glance, was for his illness the period of melancholy, of the lost sun, and of persecution. With *Impressions d'Afrique*, the sun of language is hidden within the secret; but at the heart of this night where it is maintained, it becomes marvelously fecund, causing machines and automaton corpses, incredible inventions and careful imitations to be born above itself, in the light of garden parties. During this time, life holds a promise like an imminent afterlife. Thus the work and the illness circle around their incompatibility, which binds them.

It only remains to see in this exclusion a compensatory mechanism (the work bears the burden of resolving in the imaginary the problems posed by the illness), which leads us back to Janet, and to other, lesser people.

Unless it is perceived as an essential incompatibility, nothing can ever fill the hollow core. It is also toward this void that Artaud wanted to move in his work, but from which he always found himself separated: he separated it from his work and also from himself by the work; he never stopped casting his language toward this medullary ruin, hollowing out a work which is the absence of a body of work. Paradoxically, for Roussel this hollowness is the sun, a sun which is there but which remains unattainable. It shines, but its rays remain contained within its sphere; it dazzles, but it cannot be seen through; from the core of this sun words rise, but the words cover it up and hide it; it is unique and yet it is double, and twice duplicated since it is its own mirror and nocturnal opposite.

But what is this solar emptiness if not the negation of his madness through his work, and of the work by his madness? Their mutual exclusion is along more radical lines than can be recognized within the interpretation of a unique subjective experience.

This solar void is neither the psychological background of the work (a meaningless idea) nor a theme that coincides with his illness. It *is* Roussel's linguistic space, the void from which he speaks, the absence which binds and mutually excludes his work and his madness. This void is not to be understood as a metaphor. It *is* the insolvency of words which are fewer in number than the things they designate, and due to this principle of economy must take on meaning. If language were as rich as existence, it would be the useless and mute duplicate of things; it would not exist. Yet without names to identify them, things would remain in darkness. This illuminating flaw of language was experienced by Roussel as an anguish, as an obsession, if you will. In any case, quite unique forms of experience (quite "deviant," which is to say quite disorienting) were required to expose this bare linguistic fact: that language speaks only from something essential that is lacking. From this lack is experienced the "play"—in both senses of the word (the limit and the principle simultaneously)—in the fact that the same word can designate two different things and the same sentence repeated can have another meaning. From this follows the proliferating emptiness of language, its capacity to say things, all things, to lead them to their luminous being, to place in the sun their "mute" truth, to "unmask" them. From that also follows its power to create by simple repetition things never said, nor heard, nor seen. There is the misery and the celebration of the *signifier*, and the anguish before too many and too few signs. Roussel's sun, which is always there and always "lacking," which runs the risk of dissipating itself outside, but which also shines on the horizon—that is the constitutional flaw of language, its poverty, the irreducible distance from which the light shines indefinitely. By this essential distance where language is called upon to fatally repeat itself, and things to be absurdly confused, death makes audibly clear the strange promise that language will no longer repeat itself, but will be able to repeat infinitely that which is no more.

Thus all of his work is brought back to this unity of an

"anguish" before language, to this timid psychological formulation.

It is, rather, an "anxiety" about the nature of language.
Roussel's "unreason," his derogatory play on words, his
obsessive application, his absurd inventions, communicate
doubtlessly with the reasoning of our world. Perhaps one
important thing will be clear one day: the literature of the
"absurd," from which we have recently freed ourselves,
was mistaken in the belief that it was a definition of the
consciousness, lucid and mythological at the same time, of
our condition. It was only the blind and negative side of an
experience which is common to our time, revealing to us
that it is not "meaning" which is lacking but the signifiers,
which are made significant only by what is lacking. In the
confusing play of history and existence, we simply discover
the general law of the game of significance, in which is
pursued our reasonable history. Things are perceived because words are lacking; the light of their being is the fiery
crater where language breaks down. Things, words, vision
and death, the sun and language make a unique form, the
very same one that we are. Roussel in some way has defined
its geometry. He has opened to our literary language a
strange space that could be defined as linguistic if it were
not its mirror image, its dreamy usage, enchanted and
mythic. If Roussel's work is separated from this space
(which is ours), then it can only be seen as the haphazard
marvels of the absurd, or the baroque play of an esoteric
language which means "something else." If on the contrary
his work is placed there, Roussel appears as he defined
himself: the inventor of a language which only speaks about
itself, a language absolutely simple in its duplicated being,
a language about language, enclosing its own sun in its
sovereign and central flaw. We owe the knowledge of this
invention to Michel Leiris, who prevented it from being
lost, since he transmitted it twice, in his remembrance of

Roussel, and in his novel *The Rules of the Game,* which is so essentially related to *Locus Solus.* No doubt it was necessary that from all sides of our culture be articulated this experience before all language which is anxious and animated, is extinguished and then brought back to life by the marvelous void of the signifiers. The anguish of the signified is what has made Roussel's suffering the solitary discovery of what is closest to us in our language. It makes his illness our problem. It enables us to speak of him in the context of his own language.

So you think this has justified your spending so many pages . . .

An Interview
with Michel Foucault

BY CHARLES RUAS

MICHEL FOUCAULT SET our meeting for five o'clock
at his apartment on the Rue de Vaugirard. The dignified
street of arcades along the Luxembourg Gardens quickly
becomes bourgeois with shops—bakery, greengrocer,
dairy products, delicatessen, butcher—bustling with shop-
pers and heavy with traffic at that hour. The intermittent
sunshine made the limestone buildings streaked with urban
grime suddenly glow with a golden light among the deep
luminous foliage of the sycamore trees.

His address turned out to be in a postwar white concrete
apartment block. I went through the gates, past the garage
and an intensely green garden leading to his building in the
rear. In the small lobby I stepped into a cupboard-sized
elevator which slowly took me to the top floor. When I rang
the bell, Foucault opened the door immediately, and my
first impression was one of asceticism. He was of medium
height, thin, wearing dark clothes, and his head was clean-

shaven. He appeared reserved and concentrated, but his speaking voice was warm, spontaneous, and direct, and his manner informal. He wore glasses with thick lenses, and his glance was intense, his eyes pale blue; but when he took the glasses off, he seemed completely unfocused and dreamy. His speech was often interrupted by a slight but persistent dry cough, which was the only suggestion of illness about him in September 1983.

He had looked forward to this conversation, as he was surprised by and curious about the American interest in his study of Raymond Roussel. He readily offered to assist me by clarifying any obscurity in his text. He proposed that I mark the passages I wanted to discuss in the course of working on my translation. At the same time he asked for the edited transcript of this conversation so that he could make corrections. He thought that our conversations during the course of my work could eventually make an apt postscript to the English translation of his study.

Nine months later in New York I was on my way to the post office to mail this material to him when the terrible news of his premature death caused by cancer appeared in the newspapers.

I remember being surprised the day of this interview on looking around his apartment to discover that it was one story above the roofline of the surrounding older buildings. The apartment was painted white, the floor covered by a pale tan wall-to-wall carpet; the sofa and chairs were off-white. The whole apartment seemed like a library because one wall, completely lined with bookcases, faced a wall of windows giving onto the open sky. The surrounding rooftops spread before us in a sweep of weathered tiles, slate-roofed mansards, dormers, and terraces. In every direction rose chimneys with coolie-hat coverings and round fans. With the clouds great waves of light and shadow moved across this view. In the sitting area we settled on the floor as the most comfortable place to speak, and I mentioned the wonderful view. Foucault replied that it was not the view that he valued about the apartment, but it was the clarity of light for thought that he appreciated.

M.F.: I wrote this study of Raymond Roussel when I was quite young. It happened completely by chance, and I want to stress this element of chance because I have to admit that I had never heard of Roussel until the year 1957. I can recall how I discovered his work: it was during a period when I was living abroad in Sweden and returned to France for the summer. I went to the *librairie* José Corti to buy I can't recall what book. Can you visualize that huge bookstore across from the Luxembourg Gardens? José Corti, publisher and bookseller, was there behind his enormous desk, a distinguished old man. He was busy speaking to a friend, and obviously he is not the kind of bookseller that you can interrupt with a "Could you find me such and such a book?" You have to wait politely until the conversation is over before making a request. Thus, while waiting, I found my attention drawn to a series of books of that faded yellow color used by publishing firms of the late nineteenth, early twentieth centuries; in short, books the likes of which aren't made anymore. I examined them and saw "Librairie Lemerre" on the cover. I was puzzled to find these old volumes from a publishing firm as fallen now in reputation as that of Alphonse Lemerre. I selected a book out of curiosity to see what José Corti was selling from the stock of the Lemerre firm, and that's how I came upon the work of someone I had never heard of named Raymond Roussel, and the book was entitled *La Vue*. Well, from the first line I was completely taken by the beauty of the style, so strange and so strangely close to that of Robbe-Grillet, who was just beginning to publish his work. I could see a relationship between *La Vue* and Robbe-Grillet's work in general, but *Le Voyeur* in particular. At that point José Corti's conversation came to an end, I requested the book I needed, and asked timidly who was Raymond Roussel, because in addition to *La Vue*, his other works were on the shelf. Corti looked at me with a generous sort of pity and said, "But, after all, Roussel . . ." I immediately understood that I should have known about Raymond Roussel, and with equal timidity I asked if I could buy the book since he was selling it. I was surprised or rather disappointed to find that it was expensive. José Corti probably told me that day I should read *How I Wrote Certain of My Books*. Raymond Roussel's work immediately absorbed me: I was taken by the prose style even before learning what was behind it—the process, the machines, the mechanisms—and no doubt when I discovered his process and his techniques, the obsessional side of me was seduced a second time by the shock of learning of the disparity between this methodically applied process, which was slightly naïve, and the resulting intense poetry. Slowly and systematically I began to buy all of his works. I developed an affection for his work, which remained secret, since I didn't discuss it.

The strange thing is that I met Robbe-Grillet for the first time in Hamburg in 1960 and we became friends and went to the Hamburg Fair together, going through the fun house maze of mirrors. It's the starting point of his novel *Dans le Labyrinthe*. By a mental lapse that can't have been entirely innocent on my part, I never spoke of Roussel with him, nor asked about his relationship to Roussel. That's how things stood for several years until one day during vacation I decided to write a small article on Roussel, but by then I was so absorbed by Roussel and his work that I isolated myself for two months and in fact wrote what turned out to be this book.

C.R.: If you began with the idea for an article, did other ideas that had to be explored come to you in the course of your work?

M.F.: My intention was to write an article on Roussel for *Critique* magazine. But after a few days I knew that it would be longer than an article, and I wrote without any thought of where I would publish it or how. I had discussed my work with friends who were critics, and, as a result, one day I received a telephone call from an editor asking me what I was working on.

"Oh, I'm working on a book about Raymond Roussel."

"Would you let me read it when you've completed it? Will it take you a long time?"

For once in my life I, who take such a long time with my books, could answer proudly, "I'll be finished with it very soon."

"When?" he asked.

I answered, "In eleven or twelve minutes," an answer that was completely justified by the fact that I had started typing the last page. That's the story of this book.

As for Robbe-Grillet and my lapse into silence, it was after the publication of the book that I learned that his novel *Le Voyeur* was originally entitled *La Vue* as a tribute to Raymond Roussel. It was his editor who, for completely justifiable commercial considerations, thought the title made the novel unsalable, and finally they agreed on *Le Voyeur*.

C.R.: At that time Roussel was part of your interest in the whole movement of the *nouveau roman* [new novel].

M.F.: Yes, I encountered *La Vue* by chance, and I believe I can honestly say that if I hadn't been preconditioned by the reading of Robbe-Grillet, Butor, and Barthes I would not have been capable on my own of experiencing this shock of recognition while reading *La Vue*. The chance was greater of my being interested by *How I Wrote Certain of My Books*, or by *Impressions d'Afrique*, or by any other sort of novelty than

La Vue. I really believe that this previous conditioning was necessary.

To state things in another way: I belong to that generation who as students had before their eyes, and were limited by, a horizon consisting of Marxism, phenomenology, and existentialism. Interesting and stimulating as these might be, naturally they produced in the students completely immersed in them a feeling of being stifled, and the urge to look elsewhere. I was like all other students of philosophy at that time, and for me the break was first Beckett's *Waiting for Godot,* a breathtaking performance; then reading the works of Blanchot, Bataille, and Robbe-Grillet, especially his novels *Les Gommes* [The Erasers], *La Jalousie* [Jealousy], and *Le Voyeur;* Michel Butor, Barthes' *Mythologies* [Mythologies], and Lévi-Strauss. There's an enormous difference between Bataille, Lévi-Strauss, Blanchot, and Robbe-Grillet, and I don't want to make them seem similar. For my generation they represented the break with a perspective dominated by Marxism, phenomenology, and existentialism. Having had enough of this French university culture, I left the country to go to Sweden. Had I remained within that limited horizon of my student days, under the system of classes, and that sense of the world, the end of history, it seems likely that I could have opened Roussel's book and slammed it shut with a good laugh.

C.R.: But for you the break was made with your historical study of madness. You had formulated your ideas and you were committed to a direction even before discovering Roussel.

M.F.: In fact, I was reading Roussel at the time I was working on my book about the history of madness. I was divided between existential psychology and phenomenology, and my research was an attempt to discover the extent these could be defined in historical terms. That's when I first understood that the subject would have to be defined in other terms than Marxism or phenomenology.

C.R.: I was interested by the fact that Roussel was a contemporary of Marcel Proust. If Proust's work represents the final elaboration of nineteenth-century fiction, the novelistic conventions taken to extremes, then what is Roussel's position? Cocteau called Roussel "the Proust of dreams." To me Roussel's work is the "implosion" of all novelistic conventions; he is the artist who disappears behind his work; he is hidden by the "ready-made," by the "found" convention of language that he uses to create his work.

M.F.: Yes, I think my answer will startle you because you have become "Rousselian." I have to admit that I would not dare to compare Roussel to Proust. You are right in the historical scheme of things. But I would remain very cautious about Roussel's historical place. His was an extremely interesting experiment; it wasn't only a linguistic experiment, but an experiment with the nature of language, and it's more than the experimentation of someone obsessed. He truly created, or, in any case, broke through, embodied, and created a form of beauty, a lovely curiosity, which is in fact a literary work. But I wouldn't say that Roussel is comparable to Proust.

C.R.: In the similarity to the work of Robbe-Grillet, was it his breaking with the literary conventions of his day that aroused your interest?

M.F.: There are several aspects I would comment on. First, it must be noted that Roussel belongs to a series of writers who exist in English, exist in German, exist in all languages. They are writers who have literally been obsessed with the problem of language, for whom literary construction and the "interplay of language" are directly related. I couldn't say that was a tradition because, in fact, it's a tradition that disappears with each writer as if it were so individual to each writer that it could not be transmitted but is rediscovered every time. And sometimes there are similarities that reappear. Roussel is part of that series. Of course, in the period when he was working, around 1925, he worked alone and was isolated, and, I believe, he could not be understood. There has been interest in his work only in two contexts: first, that of surrealism, with the problem of automatic writing; second, that of the *nouveau roman* in the years 1950 to 1960, a period when the problem of the relationship of literature and linguistic structure was not only a topic of theoretical speculation but also loomed large on the literary horizon.

C.R.: You had just finished your historical study of madness. Was it Roussel's psychological problems which drew your interest and made you decide to write about him at that time?

M.F.: Not at all. Once I had discovered Roussel and I learned that he had been a patient of Dr. Pierre Janet, and that his case had been written up in two pages that he quoted, I was delighted and tried to discover if anything else had been written about him in the medical literature of the day. But I could find nothing. I have to admit that my research was not extensive precisely because it was not his psychology that interested me. I don't think that I make extensive references to his psychopathology in my study.

C.R.: I assumed that your work on the history of madness would make you susceptible to Roussel.

M.F.: It's possible, but then I would say that I wasn't conscious of my interest. It wasn't because of the cultural, medical, scientific, institutional problems of madness that I became interested in Roussel. No doubt what could be said is that perhaps the same reasons which in my perverseness *[laughs]* and in my own psychopathological makeup made me pursue my interest in madness, on the one hand, made me pursue my interest in Roussel on the other.

C.R.: In your study you analyze the problem of "found" or "ready-made" language. When you referred to the surrealists' interest in automatic writing I immediately thought of their use of found objects, which has entered the mainstream of experimentation in the visual arts as well as writing. Were you challenged by the problem of how to define "found language"?

M.F.: Well, it is the interest I have in modes of discourse, that is to say, not so much in the linguistic structure which makes such a series of utterances possible, but rather the fact that we live in a world in which things have been said. These spoken words in reality are not, as people tend to think, a wind that passes without leaving a trace, but in fact, diverse as are the traces, they do remain. We live in a world completely marked by, all laced with, discourse, that is to say, utterances which have been spoken, of things said, of affirmations, interrogations, of discourses which have already occurred. To that extent, the historical world in which we live cannot be dissociated from all the elements of discourse which have inhabited this world and continue to live in it as the economic process, the demographic, etcetera, etcetera. Thus spoken language, as a language that is already present, in one way or another determines what can be said afterward either independent of or within the general framework of language. In certain of Roussel's works nothing is given at the beginning except the possibility of encountering the "already said," and with this "found language" to construct, according to his rules, a certain number of things, but on the condition that they always refer back to the "already said"—that at first delighted me, and seemed to be the interplay of literary creation starting from a cultural and historical fact. It also seemed to me that it was worth questioning.

C.R.: But the question remains, what is the relationship of the artist who will use, or starts with, a "ready-made" element in his work?

M.F.: Yes, if you wish, it's interesting to see how he distorts the fact. For example, as original as a novel might be, even if it is a *Ulysses* or a *Remembrance of Things Past,* it takes its place in a novelistic tradition and thus in the "already said" of the novel. The interesting thing about Roussel is that he doesn't use the generic matrix of the novelistic genre as the principle of development or construction. He starts with the "already said," and this "already said" can be a sentence found by chance, read in an advertisement, found in a book, or something practical. . . .

C.R.: It's his point of departure. But after writing the novels, Roussel turned to the theater with the intention of communicating more easily with the public. You would think that the theater would lend itself to the use of a "found language," since it is the genre of the world of speech and conversation.

M.F.: Well, the use of an already spoken language in the theater usually has the function of establishing a sense of verisimilitude for what is seen on stage. The familiar language placed in the mouths of the actors makes the viewer forget the arbitrariness of the situation. What Roussel did was to take a completely banal sentence, heard every day, taken from songs, read on walls, and with it he constructed the most absurd things, the most improbable situations, without any possible relationship to reality. Starting from the "already said," it's a perverse play on the usual function it exercises in the theater.

C.R.: I wanted to point out that in the novels *Impressions d'Afrique* and *Locus Solus* the fantastic beings and situations he has created are very similar to nineteenth-century games and toys. Some scenes could be descriptions of the action of those exquisite and complex automatons such as the doll who can paint Napoleon's portrait, play the piano, or write a letter. You mentioned the naïve or primitive aspect of his process. Without wanting to negate the complexity of Roussel's work, I wondered if this fundamentally private imagination was not a return to childhood, or rather a return to pure fantasy.

M.F.: It's absolutely true that there is an implicit and sometimes explicit reference to children's games, these automatons, rabbits playing drums and such, if they are taken to extremes. Only then could one say that this core of childlike imagination, the child which generally appears in all writers and is acclimated within the writing by a whole labor of elaboration, is pushed or taken toward another level of the fantastic. Roussel keeps them on their own level, in a way, and starting from the rabbit beating drums, makes the machine increasingly complex, but always remaining the same without ever passing to another register or level. There are constructions which are so intensely poetic that I don't think they are childish in themselves, but are a way of elaborating this core of childlike imagination.

C.R.: This is the aspect you analyzed in your study of his machines for the transformation of language and the hollowness, the emptiness within words. You quote Dumarsais' description of the "tropological" shift in the meaning of words as the basis of his creation. Beneath the text a secondary language is repeated, echoing within the text. Do you read Roussel listening for that second, dead-and-buried language?

M.F.: Yes, that's an interesting problem, and one of the things about Roussel that has remained completely enigmatic. It must be remembered that he didn't always use the process. In *La Vue* there is no process structuring the work. What I tried to accomplish in the book is to come to an understanding of what was the essential matrix that would take into account the texts without the process, and the texts with the process, those which obeyed the rules of the

process and those which don't. I don't know if I accomplished what I set out to do, but that was my goal. The
process poses a problem which is all the more interesting to
me because I have a student who is completely bilingual—
French-German—who is interested in Roussel, and who is
trying to write texts with a linguistic process all the more
complicated because he has to coordinate the use of two
registers: French and German. The problem with the texts
he has shown me is knowing if the interest, the complexity,
the refinement are enough to confer literary merit on the
texts produced. Working with him, reading his texts, I
couldn't help thinking of what Roussel said: "Still, one
needs to know how to use it. For just as one can use rhymes
to compose good or bad verses, so one can use this method
to produce good or bad works." Nevertheless Roussel's
work gives the distinct impression of an aesthetic control of
imaginative standards. It seemed to me that these aesthetic
criteria, considering all the possible outcomes available to
him, were inseparable from the nature of the process itself.

In the extreme, what if we didn't have *How I Wrote Certain
of My Books?* I believe it would be absolutely impossible to
reconstruct his process. I'm not referring to *Nouvelles Impressions d'Afrique,* because there the process is typographical, thus evident on the page. But in *Impressions d'Afrique* and
in *La Poussière de Soleils,* could one be unaware of a linguistic
process? There's no doubt one can ignore it. Does it dimin-
ish the quality of the work? How would Roussel be perceived by a reader who was unaware of the process? For
example, what of the American reader, or the Japanese
reader, since he has been translated into Japanese? Can
they become interested in Roussel or see the beauty of his
work without knowing that there is a process, or even
knowing that there is a process, not being able to perceive it
since the original matrix of language is not available?

C.R.: Roussel's process incorporates word play and

double entendre which are considered trivial by us, but are basic aspects of Japanese poetics. Translations of classical Japanese poetry have footnotes giving the second reading of the poem. Reading Roussel in English translation, one knows there is another aspect which is not delivered, but the surface quality of language and imagination is strikingly original and delightful.

M.F.: There is a quality of imagination which makes the work, even without knowing about the process, stand on its own. But the knowledge that there is a process throws the reader into a state of being uncertain, and even while knowing that there is no way of rediscovering the process, and even if one enjoys simply reading the text, the fact that there is a secret transforms the experience of reading into one of deciphering, a game, a more complex undertaking, more disturbing, more anxious than when one reads a simple text for the pure pleasure of it. I believe it matters to some extent knowing what was the original text that produced such and such an incident. With hard work certain sentences that served as points of departure can be clarified. A whole team of people working for years could discover the sentences that served as matrixes for each episode in Roussel's novels. But I'm not certain that it would be interesting, because it seems that aside from the beauty of the text that is pleasing in itself, the consciousness of there being a process gives the act of reading a certain tension. I'm not convinced that a knowledge of the actual text from which it starts is at all necessary.

C.R.: Were you interested in his relationship to the surrealists? He seems to have influenced artists especially.

M.F.: No, but I learned that Michel Leiris knew Roussel. I was interested in this relationship because Leiris' novel *Biffures* [Erasures] has a number of things reminiscent of Roussel. I discussed it with Leiris, but everything he had to say about Roussel is contained in his articles.

C.R.: Marcel Duchamp and other artists discuss Roussel only incidentally; there is no attempt to come to grips with his work.

M.F.: I believe that the relationship between Roussel and the surrealists was only incidental, as opposed to Leiris, who knew him. I believe the surrealists were amused and entertained by him; they saw him as a sort of Douanier Rousseau, a primitive of literature. But I don't believe the surrealists did more than orchestrate the character of Roussel, and the demonstrations defending the performances of his plays.

C.R.: How do you interpret his turning to the theater to obtain popular success?

M.F.: But, you know, for him writing was that! There's a beautiful passage in which he said that after his first book he expected that the next morning there would be rays of light streaming from his person and that everyone on the street would be able to see that he had written a book. That's the obscure desire of a person who writes. It is true that the first text one writes is neither written for others, nor for who one is: one writes to become someone other than who one is. Finally there is an attempt at modifying one's way of being through the act of writing. It is this transformation of his way of being that he observed, he believed in, he sought after, and for which he suffered horribly.

C.R.: After twenty years, can you see the place of this study in the perspective of your work and the development of your thinking?

M.F.: Those things that matter to me in a personal way, or which are important to me just as they are, I don't feel any inclination to analyze.

C.R.: From the little that is known about Roussel's life, such as his use of drugs, was opium the drug of his day?

M.F.: Oh yes, but you know the use of cocaine was al-

ready fairly widespread. It's a subject which interests me
greatly, but one which I've had to put aside—the study of
the culture of drugs or drugs as culture in the West from the
beginning of the nineteenth century. No doubt it started
much earlier, but it would come up to the present, it's so
closely tied to the artistic life of the West.

C.R.: Roussel was hospitalized for drugs rather than his
emotional problems.

M.F.: The first time that he was treated by Dr. Janet, a
great Parisian psychologist of the day, Roussel was quite
young, seventeen or eighteen, and it was due to causes that
were considered pathological, not because of his use of
drugs.

C.R.: Yet in the end when he wanted to take the cure, it
was for detoxification.

M.F.: I know that when he committed suicide in Palermo,
he had reserved rooms at the hospital in Kreuzlingen.

C.R.: The phenomenon of an artist obscured by his own
work—do you think that it is related to his sexual identity?

M.F.: Between cryptography and sexuality as a secret,
there is certainly a direct relationship. Let's take three examples: When Cocteau wrote his works, people said, "It's
not surprising that he flaunts his sexuality and his sexual
preferences with such ostentation since he is a homosexual." Then Proust, and about Proust they said, "It's not
surprising that he hides and reveals his sexuality, that he
lets it appear clearly while also hiding it in his work, since
he is a homosexual." And it could also be said about Roussel, "It's not surprising that he hides it completely since he
is a homosexual." In other words, of the three possible
modes of behavior—hiding it entirely, hiding it while revealing it, or flaunting it—all can appear as a result of
sexuality, but I would say that it is related to a way of living.
It's a choice in relation to what one is as a sexual being and
also as a writer. It's the choice made in the relationship

between the style of sexual life and the work. On reflection it should be said that because he is homosexual, he hid his sexuality in his work, or else it's because he hid his sexuality in his life that he also hid it in his work. Therefore, I believe that it is better to try to understand that someone who is a writer is not simply doing his work in his books, in what he publishes, but that his major work is, in the end, himself in the process of writing his books. The private life of an individual, his sexual preference, and his work are interrelated not because his work translates his sexual life, but because the work includes the whole life as well as the text. The work is more than the work: the subject who is writing is part of the work.

C.R.: Did your study of Roussel not lead you to other subjects that continued the pursuit of your interest?

M.F.: No, I have kept my love of Roussel as something gratuitous and I prefer it that way. I'm not a literary critic nor a literary historian, and to the extent that Roussel was unknown, except by a few people, when I wrote about him, he was not part of the great literary patrimony. Perhaps those are the reasons I had no scruples about studying him. I did not do it for Mallarmé or for Proust. I wrote about Roussel because he was neglected, hibernating on the shelves of José Corti's bookshop. I enjoyed doing it, but I am glad I never continued that work. I would have felt, not now, but in those days, that I was betraying Roussel, normalizing him, by treating him as an author like others if after writing about him I had started another study of another writer. Thus he remained unique.

C.R.: In this book there's a flight of style, a rhetorical play from chapter to chapter. Was this book different both in subject and in your approach to writing?

M.F.: Yes, it is by far the book I wrote most easily, with the greatest pleasure, and most rapidly; because I usually write very slowly, I have to rewrite endlessly, and finally there are countless corrections. I imagine it must be a complex work to read, because I belong to that category of people who, when they write spontaneously, write in a slightly convoluted manner and are obliged to simplify and clarify. In my other books I tried to use a certain type of analysis, and to write in a particular way—in short, much more deliberate, more focused. My relationship to my book on Roussel, and to Roussel's work, is something very personal, which I remember as a happy period. I would go so far as to say that it doesn't have a place in the sequence of my books. No one has tried to explain that I wrote it because I had already written a study of madness and that I would write on the history of sexuality. No one has paid much attention to this book, and I'm glad; it's my secret affair. You know, he was my love for several summers . . . no one knew it.

C.R.: You've said that you don't want to analyze your personal reactions.

M.F.: It is not a question that what I have to say can illuminate Roussel's text, but that it will eventually reveal the type of interest that a Frenchman of the nineteen sixties could bring to these texts.

C.R.: I wanted to ask you about Roland Barthes' desire at the end of his life to create a synthesis of his ideas in a work of art. He began speaking about his diaries. I wondered how you understood this change in him.

M.F.: In the *Fragments of a Lover's Discourse* he revealed himself well enough. He never discussed it directly with me. What I can tell you is that the rumors that when he died he was in a crisis, and that he wanted to die, are completely false. It happens that I was with him at the moment of the accident, and I was at the hospital where they brought him and I spoke with his doctors—the rumors are completely false.

I also happened to see him a week before his accident,

and watching him with his students at the university, I
thought, He is in his element, he's acquired the distinguished bearing of a man who is mature, serene, completely developed. I remember thinking, He'll live to be
ninety years old; he is one of those men whose most important work will be written between the ages of sixty and
ninety. I do believe that in his eyes, his critical works, his
essays, were the preliminary sketches of something which
would have been very important and interesting.

A